THE GOl

A concise history, drawing on new
material from privately printed and
manuscript sources, of the Hermetic
Order of the Golden Dawn, the cornerstone
of all modern occultism.

By the same author:

A. E. WAITE: A BIBLIOGRAPHY

Edited by the same author:

THE MAGICAL MASON
THE SORCERER AND HIS APPRENTICE

Also in this series:

THE DRUIDS: Magicians of the West
Ward Rutherford
FAIRY TALES: Allegories of the Inner Life
J. C. Cooper
MYSTICISM: The Direct Experience of God
Michael Cox
SYMBOLISM: The Universal Language
J. C. Cooper

In preparation:

ALCHEMY
Cherry Gilchrist
THE INQUISITION
Edward Burman
PYTHAGORAS AND THE PYTHAGOREANS
Ward Rutherford

THE GOLDEN DAWN

Twilight of the Magicians

by

R. A. GILBERT

THE AQUARIAN PRESS
Wellingborough, Northamptonshire

First published June 1983
Second Impression October 1983

British Library Cataloguing in Publication Data

Gilbert, R. A.
The Golden Dawn.
1. Hermetic Order of the Golden Dawn—History
135'.43   BF1623.R7

ISBN 0-85030-357-5
ISBN 0-85030-278-1 Pbk

*The Aquarian Press is part of the
Thorsons Publishing Group*

Printed and bound in Great Britain

Contents

6   *The Golden Dawn*

Foreword

Two major streams of thought have influenced the development and dissemination of Western occultism. H. P. Blavatsky and the Theosophical Society represent one stream; the other is S. L. MacGregor Mathers and the Golden Dawn. Regardless of the internecine conflicts, scandals and doctrinal schisms that occurred in both of them, all modern thinking on occult matters has been profoundly influenced by these seminal systems.

I cannot conceive of any form of occultism without thinking of Madame Blavatsky. Her influence may not be admitted or appreciated on the surface; nonetheless a little enquiry will reveal it. Even such popularizations of contemporary scientific thought such as *The Tao of Modern Physics* and *The Dancing Wu Li Masters*, which constantly make reference to Eastern religious systems, are able to do so largely because Madame Blavatsky did so much on behalf of Hindu mystical thinking. And I cannot help but remember the picture of Oppenheimer, the father of the hydrogen bomb, sitting on his desk in Padmasana reading the Bhagavad Gita.

On the other hand, there is hardly a legitimate occult order in Europe or America that has not borrowed directly or indirectly from the Golden Dawn. One has only to glance casually through Francis King's *Ritual Magic in England* to realize the enormous influence of the Golden Dawn. It was certainly not a wealthy organization; nor did it have a vast multitude of members. Yet what it stood for has percolated down through almost every level of modern occult belief.

Arthur Edward Waite was a member for a brief interval of both
these organizations. He had a rather condescending attitude
towards both Mathers and the Golden Dawn. He was indebted
more to Christian mysticism and to the traditional antecedents of
both the aforenamed groups than anything else and looked back
to the past to dredge up what he could about alchemy, the
Qabalah, the Tarot, the Rosicrucians and medieval magic. He
came to write large tomes on all of these subjects, and credit must
be given to him for whatever popularity some of them have since
achieved. I know many in the field of alchemy alone who worship
Waite for his translations of some of the basic texts in the spagyric
art. His advocacy of Christian mysticism attracted to him an
authority of the stature of Evelyn Underhill and a novelist like
Charles Williams.

Though Waite did become a member of the Golden Dawn, its
curriculum meant little to him, as indicated in his autobiography,
Shadows of Life and Thought. After the revolt at the turn of the
century he was a member of the committee that governed the
schismatic members and in consequence of this he ultimately
formed his own organization, the Fellowship of the Rosy Cross. It
employed his modifications of the basic Golden Dawn initiatory
rituals, which of course he had to transform and rewrite: his
Fellowship died when he did, in 1942. All of this is described in
Robert Gilbert's history of the Golden Dawn and in his biography
of Waite (still in preparation); interesting sidelights on the story
can also be found in his *A. E. Waite: A Bibliography.* *

This book fills in several important lacunae in the existing
historical accounts of the Order. 'The bottom of the Golden
Dawn barrel has long ago been scraped', Geoffrey Watkins wrote
to me just before he died. Be that as it may, there is much that still
needs to be said, and from a less critical viewpoint than that of
Ellic Howe in *The Magicians of the Golden Dawn* (see the Appendix
by Gerald Suster to my book *The Complete Golden Dawn System of
Magick*). Robert Gilbert's book is written more in sympathy and
sorrow for the Order's follies than with cynicism or contempt, and
it is a welcome addition to the literature that has accumulated
around the Rosicrucian legend. It also presents significant new
material.

The story of the Golden Dawn is one of vanity, gullibility and

---

* Aquarian Press, 1983

deception; and yet there inheres in it an impressive nobility, a breadth of concept and a magnanimity of both stature and structure that will persist and which is still worthy of our attention.

FRANCIS ISRAEL REGARDIE
Sedona, Arizona, October 1982

Introduction

During the course of a footnote in his seminal work *The Magicians of the Golden Dawn*, Ellic Howe refers to the printing of the manuscript 'Flying Rolls' that were circulated within the Second Order and adds: 'With the publication of these texts it might be said that the bottom of the Golden Dawn barrel has been conscientiously scraped.' From the viewpoint of the orthodox historian he is quite correct, for his own work, together with the vast mound of studies on Yeats' involvement with the Order that has built up steadily as a dismaying consequence, is more than enough to keep the most fastidious scholar happy throughout endless future incarnations. Equally, the practising magician may play for years with the rites and ceremonies given, in all their oath-breaking glory, in Israel Regardie's definitive set of published rituals. But for the more cautious, armchair student of 'rejected knowledge', and for the merely curious who wish to see what pictures appear on the pieces still missing from the Golden Dawn puzzle, there is much that remains to be told.

There may even be those who, like myself, are intrigued by Yeats' vision of the Order as a tale of lost youth. He dedicated *A Vision* to Vestigia, who was Mina Mathers, and told her of his reason for so doing:

Perhaps this book has been written because a number of young men and women, you and I among the number, met nearly forty years ago in London and in Paris to discuss mystical philosophy. You with your

beauty and your learning and your mysterious gifts were held by all in
affection, and though, when the first draft of this dedication was
written, I had not seen you for more than thirty years, nor knew where
you were nor what you were doing, and though much had happened
since we copied the Jewish Schemahamphorasch with its seventy-two
Names of God in Hebrew characters, it was plain that I must dedicate
my book to you. All other students who were once friends or friends'
friends were dead or estranged.

Who *were* those young men and women? What were they doing,
and how did they come to be doing it? And what happened to all of
them?

These are the questions that brought me to the Golden Dawn,
and so to the gradual finding of the answers. Obsessive curiosity
led me to curious documents quite distinct from the golden hoard
unearthed by Ellic Howe, and I have seen the Order principally
through the eyes of A. E. Waite, who was in the Order but not—so
long as it remained a Magical Order—of it.

Some of Waite's papers, notably his diaries, were loaned to me
by those who had the keeping of them; others were given to me by
Geoffrey Watkins, who was a constant fund of knowledge on the
Golden Dawn and its members, and Ellic Howe obtained for me
the rare opportunity of examining the 'Private Collection' of
Golden Dawn papers which had proved so valuable for his own
researches. They proved equally valuable for mine, as they
dovetailed neatly into Waite's papers and thus filled most of the
lacunae in the existing tale of the Order from 1903 to 1914. A
number of the more interesting documents from these new
sources—both ritual and historical—are printed here, as Appendices to the book, for the first time.

And, as a counterbalance to so much Waite, there is Israel
Regardie's Foreword. Dr Regardie is the very antithesis of Waite,
being practical, magical and concise with his words. It is a
privilege to be sandwiched between him and Waite: that two such
men, each great in his own Way, and each in total opposition to
the other, could find so much of lasting value in this extraordinary
Order is a wonder beyond human comprehension. That they *did*
find it is justification enough for telling the Order's tale. So let us
begin.

R. A. Gilbert
Bristol, October 1982

1. Foundation

In the beginning were the Rosicrucians—or so it would seem from the words of their followers. Far from seeing the Rosicrucians for what they were, a creation of the turmoil that followed the Reformation, nineteenth-century occultists could see them only as stemming from a vast antiquity: 'The Rosicrucians of Germany are quite ignorant of their origin; but by tradition, they suppose themselves descendants of the ancient Egyptians, Chaldeans, Magi and Gymnosophists; and this is probably true.'[1]

This yearning for a long—and distinguished—ancestry was present, too, in the latter-day Rosicrucians of the Hermetic Order of the Golden Dawn, as it was in all the occult movements and secret brotherhoods of the last century, whether respectable Freemasons claiming spiritual descent from the builders of King Solomon's Temple or Madame Blavatsky with her dubious claims for a Theosophical wisdom born in lost ages. It was possibly part of the more general desire for respectability that characterized English occultists and distinguished them from the Illuminati of the continent, who worked as much for political subversion as for spiritual enlightenment.

Such a path of revolution was abhorrent to students of the occult arts and sciences in England, whatever the tradition they followed. Thus, Ebenezer Sibly, physician and astrologer extraordinary, dedicated his massive *Illustration of the Occult Sciences* (1784) to the Freemasons, praising the 'moral rectitude and purity of design' of their Fraternity, and he took great pains to show the conformity of astrology with Christianity and to urge 'the young student in astrology' to lead an upright and sober life. Similarly, Francis Barrett, when advertising for students in the pages of his textbook of ceremonial magic, *The Magus, or Celestial Intelligencer* (1801), gave as two of the purposes of his school 'to promote the discovery of whatever may conduce to the perfection of Man' and 'the promulgation of whatever may conduce to the general happiness and welfare of mankind'. It is unlikely in the extreme that he intended this as a means of promoting illuminized radical politics.

But whether one sees it as revolutionary or respectable, the Hermetic Order of the Golden Dawn was primarily a magical order and its deepest roots lay in the magical tradition, which in England meant the Rosicrucian tradition, and in particular a certain Dr Sigismund Bacstrom.

Of Bacstrom little is known save that he was of Dutch or Scandinavian origin, had travelled widely, to Spitzbergen in 1780 and to Mauritius in 1794, and maintained a passionate interest in alchemy, collecting rare alchemical texts and performing alchemical experiments in his own laboratory with a small coterie of friends. And he was a Rosicrucian. While on the island of Mauritius Bacstrom was introduced to Louis, Comte de Chazal, who taught him alchemical secrets and initiated him into the 'Society of Rosa Crucis'. The original document, in Bacstrom's hand and certified by de Chazal, is lost, but a copy made by Frederick Hockley passed through the hands of several early members of the Golden Dawn and survives still. Their belief in the antiquity of their own Order was evidently fortified by Bacstrom's document.

In the Certificate of Admission it is made clear that the Rosicrucians are essentially Christian and primarily concerned with alchemy. As in Freemasonry, Rosicrucian brethren are sworn to eschew politics utterly, but contrary to Masonic practice 'Our Society does not exclude a worthy woman from being initiated', this provision dating, perhaps, from 1490 when the Rosicrucians 'did separate themselves from the Free-Masons'. From this, and from the fact that it had no instituted rituals, it would seem that de Chazal's Order did not derive from the German Masonic Order of the Golden and Rosy Cross, of 1777, but from the earlier alchemical Rosicrucians described by Sigmund Richter in 1710. Bacstrom gives a further account of de

Chazal in a letter of 1804 to Alexander Tilloch, one of his fellow alchemists, but makes no reference to the Rosicrucian Society. There is in fact no evidence that Bacstrom propagated the Order in England—but later occultists convinced themselves that he did simply because they wished it to have been so.

Had there been an English Rosicrucian Order in 1800 it is inconceivable that it would have been unknown to Francis Barrett, but he makes no reference to such an Order—either past or present—in *The Magus*, even though he discusses alchemy at length and promises that students of his school will 'acquire the knowledge of the Rites, Mysteries, Ceremonies and Principles of the ancient Philosophers, Magi, Cabalists, Adepts &c'. He did, however, limit the number of students to 'no greater number than twelve' and it is possible, assuming that he ever *had* any students, that they saw themselves as a Secret Fraternity and allowed others to label them as Rosicrucians.

Certainly in 1833 Godfrey Higgins refers to contemporary Rosicrucians, but these were evidently members of a Masonic Rose-Croix Chapter, for he links them with the Templars and says: 'I am not of the two Orders; I have abstained from becoming a member of them that I might not have my tongue tied or my pen restrained by the engagements I must have made on entering the chapter or encampment.'[2] In spite of the disclaimer he does not reveal anything about their structure or their rituals for he would, as a Craft Mason himself, have seen such a revelation as a betrayal of trust.

There is, in fact, no evidence whatever of a secret Rosicrucian Order working its rituals in England until the Societas Rosicruciana in Anglia was founded in 1865. According to W. Wynn Westcott, 'The revival of Rosicrucian activity in 1865 in England was the outcome of two sources; on the one hand Frater Robert Wentworth Little brought to light some Rosicrucian ritual literature which had been lying forgotten in the Record Rooms at Freemasons' Hall; on the other hand, Frater Kenneth R. H. Mackenzie brought from Austria a permission to extend to England the knowledge of certain Rosicrucian doctrines which he had received from students and initiates in that country, where he had resided for some years as an English tutor in the family of an Austrian Count.'[3] This 'Austrian Count' was one Count Apponyi, from whom Mackenzie is alleged to have received 'Rosicrucian Initiation'.

The original rules of the Society stated that 'No aspirant shall be admitted into the Society unless he be a Master Mason, and of good moral character, truthful, faithful and intelligent. He must be a man of good abilities, so as to be capable of understanding the revelations of philosophy and science; possessing a mind free from prejudice and anxious for instruction. He must be a believer in the fundamental principles of the Christian doctrine, a true philanthropist and a loyal subject.'[4] But the Golden Dawn, as we shall see, made no such restrictions. In later years Westcott was at pains to justify this distinction: 'At the Constitution of our Societas Rosicruciana in Anglia, it was decided to make it consist solely of Freemasons, although it was recognized that on the Continent many groups of Rosicrucian initiates and adepts had admitted men who were not Freemasons, and even learned women, to their grades and assemblies. This may have been a departure from the original rules of the Society, as first designed by C.R. our Founder; it is a point left undecided by the early Rosicrucian *published* literature, but there are extant documents to show that women were admitted in the 17th and 18th centuries.'[5]

And just who *were* the original Rosicrucians? They were first brought to public notice in 1614 to 1616 with the publication in Germany of a series of curious pamphlets, known as the Rosicrucian Manifestoes, entitled *Fama Fraternitatis*, *Confessio Fraternitatis* and *Chymische Hochzeit von Christian Rosencreuz* (The Chemical Wedding), and generally accepted as the work of the Lutheran scholar Johann Valentin Andreae. It has been argued, by Frances Yates, that the purpose of the pamphlets was political, and certainly they stimulated a stream of replies, both attacking and defending the mysterious Order while not producing one scrap of evidence for its real existence.

The Rosicrucian Myth, set out in the Manifestoes, is this: 'According to the "Fama Fraternitatis Benedicti Ordinis Rosae Crucis" and the "Confessio Fraternitatis R.C." the notable Mystic and Adept known as Christian Rosenkreuz, the founder of the Rosicrucian Fraternity, was born in 1378, of a noble family, and received his education in a cloister. A certain monk, P.A.L., took him as a companion on a journey to the Holy Land; they reached Cyprus, and there P.A.L. died. Christian Rosenkreuz, however, went on alone to Damascus, and to the Sanctuary of Mount Carmel where he studied with the wise men, from thence to Egypt, to Fez and then to Spain, learning in all countries the doctrines of their religion and philosophy, and their arts of medicine; and he at last settled down in South Germany about the year 1413. After several years spent in the study of the knowledge and arts so collected, C.R. chose three companions, Fratres G.V., I.A. (who, it was noted, was not a German) and I.O., and instructed them fully in the precious results of his travels, and so these four Fratres founded the 'Fraternity of the Rose and Cross'. They made a Magical Alphabet, language and dictionary, and wrote the books M (Magicon), Axiomata, Rota Mundi and Protheus; they also designed and built the house called 'Domus Sancti Spiritus' as the Home of the Fraternity. After a few years a second Circle of four other Fratres was formed; these were C.R., the son of the deceased father's brother of C.R., B., a skilful painter, G.G. and P.D., who acted as Secretary to the others. While two Fratres always remained with the Founder C.R., the others went about doing good, relieving the poor and sick and collecting further knowledge. The Fraternity then was a Society of Students of religion, philosophy and medicine, whose members sought for spiritual development and practised acts of benevolence.

'In the "Fama Fraternitatis" we read that they bound themselves by six rules:

1. To profess nothing, but to cure the sick, and that freely.
2. To wear only the usual dress of the country in which they were.
3. To assemble at the Domus S.S. once in every year on a certain day (the Festival of C.C.), or send reason for absence.
4. That each Frater should select a proper person to succeed him.
5. That the letters R.C. should be their Seal, Mark and Character.
6. To maintain the secrecy of the Fraternity for at least one hundred years.

'Frater I.O., a learned Kabalist and doctor, author of the book H., cured the young Earl of Norfolk of leprosy, and was the first member to die, and that in England. About 1450 a funeral Vault of seven sides decorated with symbols was erected for the repose of the Founder. Frater P.D. was the second to die.

'In 1457 the curious Alchymical tractate called "Chymische Hochzeit" (Chemical Wedding) was written in German by C.R. but was not then published. It narrates the attainment by him of the grade of "Eques aurei lapidis" or "Knight of the Golden Stone'.

'In 1484 the Founder and Imperator C.R. died, his body was embalmed and put into the Vault, which was closed and concealed from the members of the latest Circle of junior students.

'Frater D. was then chosen to be Magus, and after his death Frater A. at a date unknown, but he died in 1600. His successor was Frater N.N., who in 1604 discovered the entrance to the cavern and caused it to be opened, 120 years after the decease of C.R. Within the Vault was found the body carefully preserved under an Altar, and in his hand the parchment Roll called the Book T (Testamentum), also copies of other valuable books of the Fraternity, a "Vita" and an "Itinerarium" of the Founder, certain songs (*mantras*), with mirrors, glasses, bells, lamps etc. After a careful examination of all these matters the Vault was closed.

'It has been stated that this Tomb still exists, but its situation is only revealed to high Continental Adepts.'[6]

The S.R.I.A. was much more homely and concerned less with Spiritual Philosophy than with more worldly pursuits. Walter Spencer, the Masonic publisher and supplier of regalia, was greatly disappointed by them: 'The dark conspirators of this mysterious association, engaged in the painful exploration of the hermetic sciences and forbidden arts, may be *adepts* at extracting the *Elixir of Life* from Restaurant Bills of Fare, and in drawing sparkling discoveries from under the hermetic capsules of *Heidseck*, *Roederer*, and *Pommery-Greno*. In some respects their proceedings may emulate their prototype of the Middle Ages, being as profound and unintelligible a mystery to the world as to themselves. They have nothing ROSICRUCIAN—except the name.'[7]

And yet, from their ranks would come two men who *were* concerned with Spiritual Philosophy and who would, in time, create the darkly glittering splendour of the Golden Dawn.

The Rosicrucian Freemasons were not, of course, the only established body of occultists in Victorian England. Mesmerism, or Animal Magnetism, with its trances and etheric fluids, still had its followers, although the continuing refusal of the medical profession to consider its claims as a curative agent prevented any real study of its phenomena in orthodox scientific circles. It remained the property of occultists, clairvoyants and those spiritualists who were able, by mental juggling, to fit the rationalist theory of Animal Magnetism into a world-view based on the reality of spirit communion. Spiritualism itself entered Britain in the 1850s and by 1860 was well-established.

The basis of Spiritualism is a belief in the continuing, post-humous existence of the individual human being in spirit form, the ability and willingness of spirits to communicate with the living, and the existence of an orderly, happy and permanent spirit-world, in which the dead lived out their after-lives in an idealized mirror-image of contemporary society. In this spirit-world Hell had no place and many spiritualists were undoubtedly converted to the cause by a desire to evade the probability of eternal damnation that Victorian popular theology offered them. Further, Spiritualism offered the novel attraction, which no church could offer, of conversation with one's departed relatives, either by mechanical means—such as Ouija Boards and table-turning—or directly, through the voice of a medium who could offer to individuals specific messages from particular spirits.

The reaction of the churches was unanimously hostile and Spiritualistic phenomena were condemned as fraudulent or, more usually, diabolic; but however disapproving of particular practices, the churches did not deny the reality of a spiritual order, and society as a whole maintained a solid belief in the supernatural. Nor were all clerics equally hostile. Some went so far as to hold séances—the 'sittings' at which a medium, often in a trance, produces messages for those present—themselves, and one, the Revd W. Stainton Moses, was from 1872 until his death in 1892 a medium himself and the principal exponent of Spiritualist thought in England. Others were more circumspect and, whether from natural reticence or fear of episcopal wrath, carefully avoided publicity. One such group had affinities with the Rosicrucians.

The Guild of the Holy Spirit was first brought to public notice in January 1881 in the first issue of the Spiritualist journal *Light*. A brief note referred to the Guild, saying: 'The Proceedings of the Society are quite private, but it is known that the objects pursued are the study and practice of Christian Mysticism. Although the attainment of startling phenomena was not contemplated, yet some satisfactory results even of this class have been arrived at during the two months' sittings.' The third issue of *Light* carried a letter from the founder of the Guild, a 'Clergyman of the Church of England', in which he elaborated the beliefs and practices of its members: 'I have myself taken a small, private room which I have fitted up as a small chapel or oratory, and, gathering a few earnest people round me, have officiated twice a week at a simple but solemn service, in the interval of which we sit for spirit-communion . . . there are gradations in our guild; but all, from the inner to the outermost circle, are believers rather than inquirers.' He was anxious, too, to stress that the Guild guarded itself against curiosity-hunters; 'In that sense only is our society a secret one.'

It was already common to find priests, of the Anglican variety at least, within Freemasonry, but the existence of the Guild of the Holy Spirit indicates the rudiments of a willingness to be part of a hierarchical society devoted to occult pursuits on the part of clergymen without a Masonic background.

Besides communication with the departed there were other aspects of Spiritualism which were well known and enthusiastically supported not only by Spiritualists at large but also within the confines of the S.R.I.A. Clairvoyance (the ability to 'see' distant events by extra-sensory means) had been frequently demonstrated in the 1840s by proponents of Mesmerism who claimed to obtain startling results from subjects placed in a trance. Another, and far older, method of inducing clairvoyant vision was by means of gazing into a mirror or a crystal ball, both of which were employed by Frederick Hockley, the Rosicrucian Seer.

Hockley's researches into crystal vision began in 1824 and continued up to the time of his death in 1885. In 1869 he told the Committee of the London Dialectical Society how the visions were received: 'I knew a lady who was an admirable seeress, and obtained some splendid answers by means of crystals. The person who has the power of seeing, notices first a kind of mist in the centre of the crystal and then the message or answer appears in a kind of printed character. There was no hesitation and she spoke it all off as though she was reading a book, and as soon as she had uttered the words she saw, they melted away and fresh ones took their place. I have 30 volumes, containing upwards of 12,000 answers received in this way, which I keep carefully under lock and key. A crystal, if properly used, should be dedicated to a spirit.'[8] He added that 'Although I have had a crystal since 1824 I have never seen anything myself.' What he did not tell them was that he used precise magical formulae to consecrate his crystals and magic mirrors.

To his fellow Rosicrucians of the S.R.I.A. he was more forthcoming: 'After thirty years' desultory working with crystals and mirrors, I had in 1854, under spiritual instructions, prepared and consecrated a large mirror, dedicated to a spirit known to me as the C.A. [i.e. Crowned Angel], for the purpose of receiving visions and responses to metaphysical questions proposed by myself and friends.'⁹ He told them, too, how his seeress, Emma Leigh, saw the spirit of a monk who came uncalled to the crystal and related a tale of woe: he had joined a society of Rosicrucians in Rome, had learned their secrets and compiled a book of talismanic magic; then he fell into the hands of the Inquisition and was burned at the stake in 1693, learning only in the afterlife of the duplicity of the spirits he had summoned. Hockley then showed the spirit some magical talismans, and asked him if he knew anything of them. The spirit replied: 'I do know the characters. They were copied originally from some of the Rosicrucian works. There's some private libraries and manuscripts in Rome now that are kept quite secret from strangers to the order, that are full of the most curious seals and descriptions of spirits and spirit-places in their own language. You will find in my book the means of reading these.'¹⁰ These seals and their interpretations Hockley would most certainly have recorded, and as certainly they would have been seen in time by other, more ambitious, members of the S.R.I.A.

Nor was that all that Hockley recorded. In addition to his '30 volumes' of conversations with angelic beings and departed human spirits he transcribed very many unpublished manuscripts on alchemy, the Kabbalah, Talismanic Magic, and on Magical Invocations, including *Dr Rudd's Nine Hierarchies of Angels*, which contains the '18 great calls and celestial invocations of the Tables of Enoch'. Thus, within the society of Rosicrucian Freemasons were to be found the rituals, and adepts with both the knowledge and will to use them, that lay at the very heart of the magical system of the Golden Dawn.

But Spiritualism and Freemasonry were not the only currents of thought in English occultism. In 1875 a third and even more influential movement made its appearance in New York and rapidly gained world-wide, enthusiastic, and utterly uncritical support. This was the Theosophical Society, the creation of Madame Blavatsky and Colonel H. S. Olcott. Helena Petrovna Blavatsky was a remarkable person by any standards; by those of contemporary seekers after wonders and marvels she was little short of a goddess, and her departure from the Spiritualist

movement, where she had collected *en route* both fame as a
medium and the dog-like devotion of Colonel Olcott, to the more
exotic shores of Eastern occultism was inevitable. Whether or not
she had travelled in Tibet, and whether or not she served hidden
Mahatmas—indeed, whether or not such beings even exist—is
still hotly debated, but what is unquestionable is that her followers
believed implicitly that she had and that she did.

The Theosophical Society had as its objects: 'First—to form
the nucleus of an Universal Brotherhood of Humanity, without
distinction of race, creed or colour. Second—to promote the
study of Aryan and other Eastern literature, religions and sciences and vindicate its importance. Third—to investigate the hidden mysteries of Nature and the Physical powers latent in man.'[11]
In keeping with the Society's principal aim—the promotion of
Indian philosophy—both founders and the headquarters moved
to Bombay in 1879, where they gained immediate support from
both the English community and native Indians, although
Madame Blavatsky's principal work, *Isis Unveiled* (1877) was a
mixture of Indian, Gnostic, Kabbalistic and other concepts and
beliefs.

Among their supporters in India was A. P. Sinnett, the editor of
The Pioneer, and it was through his book *The Occult World* (1881),
even more than through the efforts of pioneer theosophists in
London, that Theosophy was introduced to England, where it
was seized upon by a section of the cultured middle classes who
were spiritually unsettled by religious doubts arising from the
Darwinian controversy. It is most unlikely that many of the new
theosophists understood the 'Esoteric Buddhism' thrust upon
them, but they delighted in the prospect of revelations from the
Mahatmas, Koot Hoomi and Morya; they were less enchanted by
the unprepossessing emissaries of the Masters when these arrived in the shape of Madame Blavatsky and Colonel Olcott,
neither of whom was fitted to move in English polite society. They
were even further dismayed by the more mundane revelations of
Richard Hodgson, the investigator for the Society for Psychical
Research, who reported in 1884 that the wondrous apported
letters and objects sent miraculously by the Masters to the
Theosophical Society's headquarters at Adyar were the result of
trickery. He also exposed the mechanism for faking the 'miracles'
and accused H.P.B. of fraud. The furore that followed this
exposure was the first of many in the history of the Theosophical

Society, and it undoubtedly led many members to look askance at Eastern wisdom and to seek instead a spiritual heritage nearer home.

This was readily at hand in the person of Anna Kingsford, a seeress whose 'illuminations' on the mystical interpretation of Christianity were much in vogue. She had been, in 1883 and 1884, the President of the London Lodge of the Theosophical Society but resigned because of her dislike of the emphasis on Eastern ideas and founded instead the Hermetic Society with the aim of promoting Western esoteric philosophy. This attracted many existing theosophists who agreed with her that the 'power and knowledge of an unusual kind' displayed in *Isis Unveiled* was due largely to its Western Kabbalistic elements and that these more truly represented the Theosophy of the West than did the violently anti-Christian Esoteric Buddhism of the Blavatsky camp. They were attracted, too, by the ideas of Eliphas Lévi, the French magus and self-proclaimed Kabbalist whose work was both utilized and publicized in *Isis Unveiled* and which was known to Anna Kingsford in the French texts. English Rosicrucians already knew of Lévi's occult powers from a remarkable account of a visit to him by one of their number, Kenneth Mackenzie, in 1861. In Lévi's writings they would find Tarot symbolism, the making of talismans, the theory of the Kabbalah and the concept of the Astral Light; all of which was to be part and parcel of the system of the Golden Dawn.

And among the speakers who lectured to the Hermetic Society were two—W. Wynn Westcott and S. L. MacGregor Mathers— who followed its Western path while retaining those features of the parent Theosophical Society that they found of value. As Freemasons they recognized the value of the form of Obligation that bound members to secrecy concerning certain teachings and to promise 'never to divulge certain signs and pass-words used by members of the Society for mutual recognition'. As Rosicrucians they recognized the value of superhuman hidden Masters, whose existence—real or imaginary—could be extremely useful to the leaders of an Order, whether one chose to call them Mahatmas or Secret Chiefs. As men they recognized that the time was ripe for something more splendid than Theosophy. The Golden Dawn was about to be born.

References:

1   Godfrey Higgins, *Anacalypsis, An Attempt to Draw Aside the Veil of the Saitic Isis* (1836), volume 2, p. 301.

2   ibid., volume 2, p. 723.

3   W. W. Westcott, *The Rosicrucian Society of England* (1915), p. 2.

4   R. W. Little and W. R. Woodman (eds.), *The Rosicrucian*, No. 1 (1868), p. 7.

5   Westcott, *op. cit.*, p. 3.

6   Westcott, *Data of the History of the Rosicrucians* (1916), pp. 3–5.

7   Spencer, *Freemasonry: Its Outward and Visible Signs* (1880), p. 96.

8   *Report on Spiritualism* of the Committee of the London Dialectical Society (1873), p. 184.

9   Frederick Hockley, 'Evenings with the Indwellers of the World of Spirits', in *The Rosicrucian and Masonic Record*, New Series, No. 6 (1877), p. 223.

10 ibid., p. 230.

11 *Rules of the Theosophical Society* (1882), p. 5.

2. Creation

On 8 December 1888 an enquirer signing himself Gustav Mommsen posed this question in the magazine *Notes and Queries*: 'Johann F. Falk succeeded to the directorate of a secret society of students of the Kabbalah about 1810, in London I believe. Its name was "Chabrah Zereh aur bokher", as nearly as Hebrew can be put into English. The late Eliphaz [sic] Lévi, of Paris, was concerned in it later on. Is this society still in existence?' An answer was soon forthcoming and appeared in February 1889: 'The Order of mystics which gave Eliphaz Lévi (Abbé Constant), his occult knowledge, and of which Johann Falk was at one time the Lecturer on the Kabbalah in London, is still at work in England. It is not a Masonic order, and there is no distinction between men and women students. The greatest privacy is maintained, and some knowledge of Hebrew is essential, but the whole course of study and experiment is so abstruse and complex that the membership is very limited as to numbers, and the proceedings have no public interest. Its true name is only told to initiates, and the few outsiders who have heard of its existence only know the society as "The Hermetic students of the G.D."' It was signed by W. Wynn Westcott, who quite unnecessarily gave his address—396 Camden Road, London, N.

Or was it unnecessary? It is difficult to imagine anything that would have excited budding occultists more than to tell them that the Kabbalistic School which had trained Eliphas Lévi survived and flourished in England. It is also difficult to imagine that both

question and answer were anything but a 'put-up job', for it was
Westcott who invented the Golden Dawn's Hebrew name, and
Westcott alone who adopted the mannerism of ending Lévi's
christian name with a 'z'. And it was Westcott, as we shall see, who
invented rather more than just a name for the Order.

By 1888 Eliphas Lévi was well known to the occult minded
public, for he had been the subject of extravagant praise from
both Madame Blavatsky and Anna Kingsford, his *Paradoxes of the
Highest Science* had appeared in *The Theosophist*, and A. E. Waite
had published, in translation, an anthology of his Kabbalistic and
Magical writings under the title of *The Mysteries of Magic*. He was
also conveniently dead and so could not dispute the claims made
upon his behalf.

In contrast to Lévi, William Wynn Westcott was little known,
save to his fellow Rosicrucians of the S.R.I.A. and to the members
of Anna Kingsford's Hermetic Society, amongst whom he was
respected as an authority on Alchemy, and on Kabbalistic and
Hermetic Philosophy. Westcott was born in 1848, orphaned at an
early age, but received a good education and qualified as a
medical practitioner in 1871. He practised with his uncle at
Martock in Somerset, where he was made a Mason in 1872; but by
1880 he had moved to London, taken up his various occult
pursuits and joined the Rosicrucian Society.

For the next ten years he advanced steadily both in medicine
and in Hermeticism: in 1881 he became a Deputy Coroner, in 1882
Secretary General of the S.R.I.A.; by 1892 he was Coroner for
North-East London, and in the same year was elected Supreme
Magus of the Rosicrucians. And during that same decade he
made the discovery that was to bring him a doubtful kind of
immortality.

In 1887, according to his own story, Westcott acquired and
translated a strange manuscript that had been written in a cipher,
to which, fortunately, he possessed the key. The manuscript
contained the rough draft of a series of initiatory rituals of a
quasi-Masonic nature. It also contained the name and address of
a German Adept to whom Westcott wrote and from whom he
received the authority to found the Isis-Urania Temple of 'Die
Goldene Dammerung'; in Westcott's English this became the
Golden Dawn.

The tale of the magical manuscripts upon which the Order
based its very being has been told in countless versions, no two of

which agree entirely. Some versions are for the credulous, others for the sceptical; of the latter, Arthur Machen's is perhaps the most succinct:

A gentleman interested in occult studies was looking round the shelves of a second-hand bookshop, where the works which attracted him were sometimes to be found. He was examining a particular volume—I forget whether its title was given—when he found between the leaves a few pages of dim manuscript, written in a character which was strange to him. The gentleman bought the book, and when he got home eagerly examined the manuscript. It was in cipher; he could make nothing of it. But on the manuscript—or, perhaps, on a separate slip laid next to it—was the address of a person in Germany. The curious investigator of secret things and hidden counsels wrote to this address, obtained full particulars, the true manner of reading the cipher and, as I conjecture, a sort of commission and jurisdiction from the Unknown Heads in Germany to administer the mysteries in England. And hence rose, or re-arose, in this isle the Order of the Twilight Star. Its original foundation was assigned to the fifteenth century.

I like the story; but there was not one atom of truth in it. The Twilight Star was a stumer—or stumed—to use a very old English word. Its true date of origin was 1880—1885 at the earliest. The 'Cipher Manuscript' was written on paper that bore the watermark of 1809 in ink that had a faded appearance. But it contained information that could not possibly have been known to any living being in the year 1809, that was not known to any living being till twenty years later. It was, no doubt, a forgery of the early 'eighties. Its originators must have had some knowledge of Freemasonry; but, so ingeniously was this occult fraud 'put upon the market' that, to the best of my belief, the flotation remains a mystery to this day. But what an entertaining mystery; and, after all, it did nobody any harm.[1]

Westcott himself claimed to have obtained the cipher manuscript from the Revd A. F. A. Woodford, an elderly Masonic scholar who died, conveniently for Westcott, at the end of 1887 before the Golden Dawn was announced to the world. In fact, it almost certainly came from within the Rosicrucian Society, of which Woodford was not a member, and was probably the work of Kenneth Mackenzie, whose *Royal Masonic Cyclopaedia* (1877) contained a list of Rosicrucian grades that matched the Golden Dawn grade structure almost perfectly. Mackenzie insisted that this list was his own work, but he had lifted it intact from a

German Rosicrucian text of 1781—a text that would have been
known to Westcott also.

The cipher itself, which is alchemical in origin, would have
posed few problems for Westcott, who was familiar with old
alchemical and magical texts and was well aware of Trithemius'
Polygraphiae—the book which contains the cipher's key. Translating it he found that it was in English, although written from
right to left, that it allowed for both male and female initiates, and
that it needed considerable improvement before the rituals could
be worked. He further found that the German Adept was the
'famous soror' Sapiens Dominabitur Astris of Nuremberg, whose
real name was Anna Sprengel.

In her 'reply' to Westcott's initial letter, Anna Sprengel distri-
buted occult largesse wholesale: Westcott was raised to the status
of Adeptus Exemptus ($7° = 4°$), he was authorized to establish a
new Temple in England and to choose two companions to be his
co-Chiefs. A further letter gave him the right to sign Fraulein
Sprengel's motto on her behalf on any papers necessary for the
founding and working of other Temples. Westcott had wished for
an Adept and, as with all wishes made true, he had found one in
the realm of Fairyland. W. B. Yeats recorded her true nature in
his allegorical account of the founding of the Order: 'Then an old
woman came, leaning upon a stick, and, sitting close to them, took
up the thought where they had dropped it. Having expounded the
whole principle of spiritual alchemy, and bid them found the
Order of the Alchemical Rose, she passed from among them, and
when they would have followed was nowhere to be seen.'[2]

Disappearance, however, was not sufficient for Westcott, and
once Anna Sprengel had served her purpose and written him her
five letters,[3] he killed her off. Her death, on 20 July 1890, was duly
reported by another German Adept, who added the information
that other Chiefs objected to corresponding with Westcott. He
was now free to carry on the Order without interference from his
nominal and non-existent superiors in Germany.

As his co-Chiefs of Temple No. 3 (Number 1 was Sapiens
Dominabitur Astris' fictitious Licht, Liebe, Leben Temple, and
Number 2 the equally fictitious Hermanubis Temple of the
unknown Englishmen who held the cipher manuscript before
Woodford's alleged discovery of it) Westcott selected Dr W. R.
Woodman, Supreme Magus of the S.R.I.A., of whom little is
known and less need be said, and another Rosicrucian Mason,

Samuel Liddell MacGregor Mathers. To Mathers, Westcott entrusted the task of reconstructing the cipher rituals so that they could be worked. He had already ensured, with Mathers' help, that the Order would be well publicized.

The first step in promoting the Order came in February 1888, with a letter from Mathers to the Editor of *Light*. Ostensibly this was in reply to a critical article on Eliphas Lévi, but it was effectively a puff for the newborn Golden Dawn: 'Eliphas Lévi was indeed an Initiate of the Kabbalah, a member of the Fraternity of the Rosy Cross, and of other kindred orders, and was acknowledged as a Brother by those who know.'[4]

On the first of March the Warrant for the Isis-Urania Temple of that same 'Fraternity of the Rosy Cross', under its new name of the Order of the Golden Dawn in the Outer, was drawn up and signed. It is a somewhat introverted document, for the Three Chiefs of the Second Order, Deo Duce Comite Ferro (Mathers), Sapiens Dominabitur Astris (Westcott in his *alter ego* of Anna Sprengel) and Vincit Omnia Veritas (Woodman), deputed themselves, under their respective First Order mottoes of 'S Rioghail Mo Dhream, Quod Scis Nescis (Westcott as himself, although he normally used the motto Sapere Aude) and Magna est Veritas et Praelavebit, 'To constitute and rule the Isis-Urania Temple No. 3'. This they duly did, their first act being the initiation of nine members at the Spring Equinox Ceremony that same March.

The first of the new initiates was Miss Mina Bergson, the sister of the philosopher Henri Bergson, soon to be Mrs Mathers and thus central to the entire story of the Order. Mathers himself is an enigma. He was born in 1854, educated at Bedford Grammar School and lived with his widowed mother at Bournemouth— where he was made a Mason in 1877—until her death in 1885, when he moved to London to dedicate himself to Hermetic Philosophy, magical practice and an obsession with his fancied Jacobite ancestry. His later history is one of growing eccentricity, of delusions both of persecution and grandeur, and of paranoia: it is also, to a large extent, the history of the Order itself.

But for all his oddity, Mathers' friends and enemies alike admitted the extent of his learning, even if they did not admire it. A. E. Waite described him as a 'comic Blackstone of occult lore' and recalled him pursuing his occult quests in the British Museum, all day and every day, absorbing knowledge rather than sifting it, for Waite looked upon Mathers as having 'an utterly uncritical mind'. A similar judgement was made by W. B. Yeats, who said of Mathers that he had 'much learning, but little scholarship, much imagination and imperfect taste'. Against this, J. W. Brodie-Innes spoke of 'his wonderful learning in strange bypaths of knowledge' and said: 'Of his scholarship it is not for me to speak, so far was it beyond my own', and Brodie-Innes *was* a scholar.

Brodie-Innes also claimed for Mathers the 'loyalty and affection' in later days of members of the Golden Dawn, a claim patently false and on a par with Mina Mathers' mendacious assertion that 'In 1888, after the publication of the *Qabalah Unveiled*, my husband started the working of his esoteric school . . . Dr Woodman and Dr Wynn-Westcott aided in the administrative side of this school and its teaching to a certain extent.'[5] Mathers' role in building the Golden Dawn was undoubtedly a crucial one, but he did not found the Order; it was Westcott who blended fantasy with reality and created it from nothing.

And he was determined that it should be the only Rosicrucian Order. At first it was not, for there was also 'a certain bogus occult society known by the name of "Ros. Crux. Fratres", or the Order of the "Dew and the Light", whose headquarters are at Keighley, and which has members in almost every town in England'.[6] This Yorkshire Society was exposed in the pages of *Lucifer* by 'One who has been duped'—probably at the instance of Westcott and Mathers, who used the exposure to publicize, as true Rosicrucian Orders, both the S.R.I.A. *and* the Golden Dawn. At the end of Mathers' letter dissociating the S.R.I.A. from spurious Rosicrucian Orders, he stated: 'The Secretary General of the Society, Dr Wynn Westcott, Hon. IX., will be pleased to give further information as to the true status of any claimant to high rank among the Rosicrucians: letters should be sent to the High Council Offices, 396, Camden Road, London.'[7] Having given the address, he then added this pompous statement about the Golden Dawn itself: '*The Hermetic Students of the Rosicrucian G.D. in the Outer*. The chiefs of the Second order fearing that the proceedings of certain men in the Northern Counties of England may by exhibition of pretended powers and Rosicrucian dignities lead students away from the Higher Paths of Mysticism, into Goetic practices, desire that all Fratres and Sorores of the G.D. will accordingly warn the unwary and uninitiated that no such persons hold any warrant from us, nor possess our ancient and secret knowledge. Given forth from the M[ountain] A[biegnos] of Sapiens Dominabitur Astris. Deo duce comite Ferro. Non omnis moriar. Vincit omnia veritas. Published by order of the above: Sapere Aude: Cancellarius in Londinense.'[8]

Further correspondence between David Lund of the 'Dew and the Light', the nameless Dupe (who may have been T. H. Pattinson of the Golden Dawn), and Westcott himself merely exchanged abuse about their various orders. The Dupe said of the Keighley adepts that:

They profess to teach students of the occult the following subjects, viz.:— 1st, Alchemy; 2nd, The Philosophy of Life; 3rd, the Divine Art of Astrology; 4th, the Herbs and their value as medicines; and 5th, the Astral influences. But when the student becomes a member, he finds that they are incapable of teaching any of these subjects, and that they have imposed upon him with mysterious words and high-sounding phrases. They profess to be in the possession of much knowledge which they cannot give to the student, until he has attained to their state, and this knowledge is copied from books, which they either possess, or borrow or steal, and when they descend to originality it is simply one mass of error and nonsense. One man who is more learned in Black Magic than the rest, tries to project himself on the astral plane and beget astral children.[9]

Their learning, he says, they also derive 'from Elementals and Spirit-guides'; even worse, 'the members boast that they sacrifice kids and they have already sacrificed two'. Worst of all, 'when the members meet in Lodge, they transact no business except talking rubbish, if that can be called business'.

To the sceptic this may sound very like the business of the Golden Dawn itself, but whatever their other faults, Westcott and Mathers were honest Hermetic scholars and were both able and willing to teach their members, even though the knowledge imparted was—in the First Order—little more than Kabbalistic, Alchemical and Astrological symbolism. This meagre fare was supplemented by instruction in Geomantic and Tarot divination, Tattwa vision and the Pentagram Ritual, which 'was taught to the Neophyte immediately after his initiation in order that he might "form some idea of how to attract and come into communication with spiritual and invisible things"'.[10] An account of the practical and theoretical work of both the First and Second Orders is given in Chapter 5 of this book, but the texts quoted there and in the

Appendices do not exhaust the activities of the Order; the reader seeking full enlightenment, or more complete confusion, is advised to seek it out in the pages of Israel Regardie's comprehensive study.

By March 1890, after countless aeons on the astral planes and two years in the real world, all opposition was routed and the Hermetic Order of the Golden Dawn ruled supreme over a band of some seventy-eight Rosicrucians scattered about the country and gathered into its three Temples. The siting of these Temples indicates the Order's dependence upon the S.R.I.A. for a continuing supply of members. Isis-Urania in London was, of course, the hub of the Rosicrucian universe and held fifty-five members in its orbit, while Osiris at Weston-super-Mare claimed eight and Horus at Bradford thirteen, including one woman. Bradford contained numerous Freemasons from the York College of the S.R.I.A. as well as many active Theosophists; but Weston-super-Mare owed its Temple solely to the enthusiasm of its Borough Treasurer, Benjamin Cox, an ardent occultist who was active in the Rosicrucian Society's Bristol College and managed to draw half-a-dozen of his fellow Freemasons into the Golden Dawn's seaside Temple. It was never a great success, and when Cox died in 1895 his Temple died with him.

Each of the three Temples was organized on the same principles, having the same hierarachical structure and working identical rituals. The rituals were those devised by Mathers, on the basis of Westcott's cipher manuscript, for the $0° = 0°$ Neophyte Grade and for the successive grades of Zelator ($1° = 10°$), Theoricus ($2° = 9°$), Practicus ($3° = 8°$) and Philosophus ($4° = 7°$), which were the only grades given in the manuscript. These five constituted the whole of the First Order grades and to them Westcott added three more for the Second Order—Adeptus Minor ($5° = 6°$), Adeptus Major ($6° = 5°$) and Adeptus Exemptus ($7° = 4°$)—and a further three for the Secret Chiefs of the Third Order who dwelt solely on the astral plane: Magister Templi ($8° = 3°$), Magus ($9° = 2°$) and Ipsissimus ($10° = 1°$). All save the highest were drawn directly from the structure of the S.R.I.A. and indirectly from the eighteenth-century German Masonic Order of the Gold and Rosy Cross.

It was essential to Westcott's scheme of things to have ten grades, for they were intended to represent the ten Sephiroth, or Emanations, of the Kabbalistic Tree of Life, the first grade, $1° =$

10°, standing for the tenth and lowest Sephira, Malkuth, and the unattainable tenth grade, $10° = 1°$, standing for Kether, the first of the Sephiroth. Entry to the Second Order was at first by examination on the basis of the Order's theoretical teaching and was solely to the $5° = 6°$ degree of Adeptus Minor. Only the Three Chiefs, Westcott, Woodman and Mathers, had attained the level of Adeptus Exemptus—having awarded it to themselves at the outset.

It was mandatory upon every member of the Golden Dawn to take a new name in the form of a motto, usually in Latin, upon entering the Order. This was then the secret name by which he or she was known within the Order; but although it was permissible, it was very rare for members to change their mottoes when they advanced to the Second Order. The Three Chiefs, however, had collected new and unpublicized mottoes to go with their $7° = 4°$ grades; an astute move, for it enabled them to hide the fact that the Secret Chiefs of the Second Order were also the self-appointed officers of the Isis-Urania Temple in the Outer.

Members were free to choose their own mottoes, provided that they were not already in use, and most were mundane, Latin and eminently worthy. Some were Hermetic Axioms, a few were in other languages—Gaelic, Greek, Hebrew or German—and some, such as Blackden's 'Ma Wahanu Thesi' and Pamela Carden's 'Shemeber', were quite incomprehensible. It was also common practice to contract the motto to its initials or to use only the first word when referring to fellow members; thus Vestigia was Mina Mathers' name rather than the full 'Vestigia Nulla Retrorsum' and Yeats' 'Demon est Deus Inversus' became simply 'Demon'. Westcott was invariably S.A. rather than 'Sapere Aude'.

But before they obtained their mottoes, before even entering the Order, candidates had to be approved by the Chiefs—who did not approve of Spiritualist mediums or of any others who 'allow themselves to fall into a complete Passive Condition of Will'—and were made to sign a Pledge of secrecy in all things concerning the Order and an acceptance of the 'Ordinances of the First Order of the G.D. in the Outer'. They also had to pay a ten shilling admission fee, an annual subscription of 2s 6d and the cost of rituals and lectures.

Once initiated, the Neophyte found himself in a Temple ruled by Three Chiefs who acted as Imperator, Cancellarius (or

Secretary), and Praemonstrator (whose task was to oversee the studies of the members and to ensure that they learned and correctly performed the rituals). The rituals themselves were carried out by other officers whose titles—Hierophant, Hiereus, Hegemon, Kerux, Stolistes and Dadouchos—were taken from the Eleusinian Mysteries and who had themselves attained the grade appropriate to their status. Their functions would have been explained to the Neophyte in the course of his initiation (see Appendix A). But however impressive the officers were and however awe-inspiring the rituals, they were not magical rituals, and the Rosicrucians of the Golden Dawn, although they were loth to admit it, wanted magic. Mathers, alone among the Secret Chiefs, recognized the members' needs and his genius for creating rituals ensured that it was not long before they got what they wanted; but—as is the way with magic—it brought untold trouble in its wake.

References:
1 Arthur Machen, *Things Near and Far* (1923), pp. 152–153.
2 W. B. Yeats, *Stories of Red Hanrahan: The Secret Rose: Rosa Alchemica* (1913), p. 215.
3 See Appendix B.
4 *Light*, Vol. 8, No. 370, p. 55.
5 S. L. M. Mathers, *The Kabbalah Unveiled* (1926), Introduction by Mrs Mathers, pp. viii–ix.
6 *Lucifer*, Vol. 4, No. 22 (June 1889), p. 349.
7 ibid. p. 350.
8 ibid. p. 351.
9 ibid. p. 349.
10 Israel Regardie, *The Golden Dawn*, Vol. 1 (1937), p. 75.

3. Action

Before 1892 the Order was without magic, and for the first four years of their Rosicrucian lives the members were Spiritual Philosophers. As Mathers told Yeats: 'We only give you symbols ... because we respect your liberty.'[1] When he did give them something other than symbols it was the fully-fledged workings of the Second Order, which was run by Mathers for Mathers— liberty, along with equality, had disappeared.

Advancement to the Adeptus Minor Grade of $5 = 6$ took place in the Outer Order, but it was by means of an examination and it was, to all intents and purposes, a purely honorary degree that gave the holder little more than the right to act as Hierophant at Outer Order ceremonies. To many members the Outer Order gave little enough anyway; Arthur Machen's experience of it was not entirely untypical: 'I must say that I did not seek the Order merely in quest of odd entertainment ... I had experienced strange things—they still appear to me strange—of body, mind and spirit, and I supposed that the Order, dimly heard of, might give me some light and guidance and leading on these matters. But, as I have noted, I was mistaken; the Twilight Star shed no ray of any kind on my path.'[2]

This changed when Mathers returned from Paris, where he had gone seeking enlightenment, in the autumn of 1891. He had met, or so he said, a high Adept, Frater Lux e Tenebris—later alleged to have been one Dr Thiessen—who gave him all the materials for constructing a Second Order ritual. By December the Ritual was complete and a Vault was being constructed at Thavies Inn, off Holborn Circus. The first initiation took place on 7 December and was described by Waite from the account that the candidate, Annie Horniman (Fortiter et Recte), gave him many years later: 'Fortiter took the 5 = 6 Ceremony at Thavies Inn. The roof was not on the Vault and the painting on the Crook and the Scourge was wet. Fortiter was the first candidate to take it, preceding Sapientia because she was going abroad.'³ Possibly Miss Horniman was made the first initiate—when the Vault was far from ready—out of gratitude.

She had taken a liking to Mina Bergson and had persuaded her father to employ Mathers as the curator of his private ethnographical museum (now the Horniman Museum) at Forest Hill in South London so that he and Mina could be married. The Mathers now lived at Stent Lodge, Forest Hill, and used their home for ceremonies—Waite was initiated there and Yeats introduced to magic at Stent Lodge—until 1891, when Mathers lost his job as curator and his home with it. Annie Horniman now helped them financially, enabling Mina to study art in Paris, where Mathers soon joined her to study magic. Without Fortiter's generosity the whole Second Order would have been long delayed; she had well-earned her priority for Initiation.

The ceremonies of the Second Order were startling and spectacular, displaying Mathers' ritual talents to the full—even the name, for as a new Order it required a new name, was grandiose: Ordo Roseae Rubeae at Aureae Crucis, although this did no more than reflect the Order's Rosicrucian nature. The Adeptus Minor Ritual was a re-enactment of the death and resurrection of Christian Rosenkreuz, involving the symbolic crucifixion of the candidate and the rising of the Chief Adept from the tomb, or pastos, within the seven-sided vault that was central to the ritual. Both vault and tomb were intricately painted with a multitude of occult symbols, all in their correct colours, and the candidate received instruction in their meaning from the three Adepts who initiated him. The effect on candidates must have been overwhelming; even the normally cynical Waite was impressed: 'It could not be denied that the culminating Grade, as the system was then developed, had the root-matter of a greater scheme than had ever dawned in the consciousness of any maker of Masonic Degrees under any Grand Lodge or Chapter, Conclave or Preceptory, in the whole wide world.'⁴

Mathers was not content with the Christian content of Rosicrucian symbolism and introduced many Egyptian elements which were yet extremely effective. The full text of the ritual, with a description of the vault, is given by Regardie,[5] but the following notes, made by W. A. Ayton some time after his initiation in September 1892, reflect an understanding—or misunderstanding—of the ritual at the time it was created. The odd conclusion is some eclectic aberration of Ayton's own:

5 = 6 Ritual

Important to know by heart.

First Point. End of Second Adept's prayer 'O God the vast one' &c &c
Second Point. Second Adept's prayer in the V[aul]t & Chief Adept in Pastos speech, beginning: 'Buried with that sight.'
Third Point. Whole of Ritual up to the explanation of the mystic number, name &c.

I am the Way (Tiphereth)
the truth (Geburah)
& the life (Chesed)
No man cometh unto the Father but by me (Chokmah)
I am purified
I have passed thro' the gates of darkness into Light
I have fought upon earth for good, I have entered into the invisible, I have finished my work.
I am the Sun shining in his rising, I have passed thro' the hour of cloud & night (Meshamah in Binah)
I am Ammon the concealed one, the opener of the day. I am Osiris Osorronophris, the justified One (Chiah in Chokmah)
I am the Lord of Life triumphant over death. There is no part of me that is not of the gods. (Yechidah in Kether)
I am the preparer of the pathway. The rescuer unto the sight. Out of the darkness let the Light arise.
(Behold, I was blind, now, I see)
I am the Dweller in the invisible. I am the reconciler with the ineffable. Let the white brilliance of the Divine Spirit descend.
I AM the All-sustainer.
I AM the All-wise.
I have no stain,

Sakia Muni
The Buddhist of Tibet.

Scarcely had the paint finally dried upon the vault than it was dismantled and moved to new premises in Clipstone Street, not far from Oxford Circus, where it sat and watched over a procession of initiates duly awed by its multi-coloured splendour and by the spectacle of Mathers in glittering Egyptian robes rising from the tomb of Christian Rosenkreuz. Nor were initiations all that it witnessed; the Second Order required its members to enter their names in a diary when they visited the vault and to record their magical (or other) activities. In the two diaries that survive for 1892 and 1893 it is recorded that over a period of eighteen months thirty initiations took place, numerous magical invocations were carried out and a number of Adepti Minores made and consecrated their magical instruments in the vault.

Mathers was busy flying (metaphorically) between London and Paris, gaining magical knowledge from the Secret Chiefs and cadging money from Annie Horniman. He was also engaged in a grandiose dream about his fictitious Highland ancestry and dabbling in reactionary politics in France, although magic remained his primary concern. The Secret Chiefs were undoubtedly real to him—had he not met them in the flesh in the Bois de Boulogne?—and he made the following statement about them to his Adepti Minores in the course of a long and paranoid 'Manifesto', which he issued to the Order in 1896 (the 'Manifesto' demanded the submission to his will of all the members of the Second Order, who were becoming unhappy with his autocratic rule and suspicious of the Secret Chiefs):

Concerning the Secret Chiefs of the Order, to whom I make reference and from whom I have received the Wisdom of the Second Order which I have communicated to you, I can tell you *nothing.*

I do not even know their earthly names.

I know them only by certain mottoes.

I have *but very rarely* seen them in the physical body; and on such rare occasions the *rendezvous was made astrally by them* at the time and place which had been astrally appointed beforehand.

For my part I believe them to be human and living upon this earth; but possessing terrible superhuman powers.[6]

Their terrible powers were endorsed fully by Mathers' more loyal—and, some would say, credulous—followers. Among these was Dr Edward Berridge, a homoeopathic physician and supporter of the esoteric sexual doctrines of Thomas Lake Harris, which he attempted to propagate within the Golden Dawn (Annie Horniman condemned him for this as 'impure and mischievous'). Within the Order he was known by his motto of 'Resurgam', and under this name he contributed an article on the Rosicrucians to A. E. Waite's journal *The Unknown World*; it contained the following remarkable claim regarding the Order's private papers: 'Doubtless the Higher Chiefs take means for removing any important MSS from those whom they see about to become incapacitated either by illness or death. As for treachery, it is not likely that any very important secrets would be given to a member until his fidelity was thoroughly assured; and every initiate of an Occult Order knows that his wilful perjury would be followed by unpleasant consequences—*possibly a Coroner's inquest, and a verdict of 'Death from Syncope'.*[7]

At the time this appeared Waite was not a member of the Golden Dawn, but he undoubtedly knew what was going on. He had joined the Order early in 1891, took the Theoricus and Practicus Grades as a 34th birthday present, added the $4 = 7$ in April 1892 and left shortly afterwards, taking with him his motto of 'Sacramentum Regis Abscondere Bonum Est' (It is good to keep the secret of the King)—appropriately, as it happened, for, as he said, 'I retired or rather demitted without explanation; and if I thanked my stars that in so doing I missed but little, it is more than probable that the Hermetic Order of the G.·.D.·. missed even less. I had no grist in my granaries for a mill of that kind.'[8] Waite was re-admitted in 1896, entered the Second Order and waited for his time to come.

The Order continued to expand: in Edinburgh the Amen-Ra Temple was consecrated in 1893 and the Scottish Adepts promptly erected their own Second Order vault; Mathers, or Deo Duce Comite Ferro as we should call him in a Second Order context, set up a new Temple in Paris, Ahathoor No. 7, and asked Annie Horniman to consecrate it in January 1894; and the Secret Chiefs were providing examination material for the New Grade of Theoricus Adeptus Minor. But all was not well.

Annie Horniman was growing increasingly unhappy with Mathers' constant demands for money and was concerned over his political involvements. His letters to her, and to others about her, were rude and belligerent, and finally she had had enough. In September 1896 she resigned as sub-Praemonstratrix of Isis-

Urania and told Mathers that there would be no more money. He promptly issued his 'Manifesto', to which she meekly submitted—but she remained firm over the money and the infuriated Mathers expelled her from the Order.

The other members were appalled by Mathers' actions and petitioned for her reinstatement, only to have their request flung back at them by their unforgiving and undemocratic Chief. Soon after they suffered another loss with the resignation of Westcott, who had become Vice-Imperator of Isis-Urania. He was told bluntly by the authorities to cease his occult activities: 'It had somehow become known to the State Officers that I was a prominent official of a society in which I had been foolishly posturing as one possessed of magical powers—and that if this became more public it would not do for a Coroner of the Crown to be made shame of in such a mad way.'[9] Or, as Aleister Crowley put it, 'Did they further intimate to Dr Westcott that he was paid to sit on corpses, not to raise them; and that he must choose between his Coronership and his Adeptship?'[10]

Whether Mathers engineered this discovery by the authorities or not is a matter for conjecture, but he was now in a position of undisputed power. He was also turning his attention to ritual magic of a dangerous kind. In 1896 he began work on the translation of a French magical text that was finally published in 1898 as *The Book of the Sacred Magic of Abra-Melin the Mage*. This work had been fraught with peril; Mathers sent the translation to F. L. Gardner, who was arranging for its publication, and warned him to be careful with both text and artwork: 'The *shape* of the Casket presented by the head of the lower triad of Demons in the drawing was altered completely in the pencil sketches, and that by no mortal hand.'[11]

No Abra-Melin demons came to bother the Order, but one of their disciples did. On 18 November 1898 a Neophyte was initiated into the Outer Order at Mark Masons' Hall, where the meetings were regularly held, who took the name of Frater Perdurabo. In the outside world he was Aleister Crowley and was soon to be a thorn in the flesh of Mathers, whom he was to rival, and eventually to surpass, in magical prowess.

By 1900, as their Chief's autocratic behaviour steadily grew more intolerable, the members in London decided that closing down Isis-Urania was the only course to follow. Mathers was furious and refused to consider closure, suggesting in a letter to

Florence Farr that the existing officers were welcome to resign. In the same letter he dropped a bombshell; referring to Westcott—whom he feared would form a schismatic Order—he said:

> He has NEVER been *at any time* either in personal or in written communication with the Secret Chiefs of the Order, he having *either himself forged or procured to be forged* the professed correspondence between him and them, and my tongue having been tied all these years by a previous Oath of Secrecy to him, demanded by him, from me, before showing me what he had either done or caused to be done or both. You must comprehend from what little I say here, the *extreme gravity* of such a matter, and again I ask you, both for his sake and that of the Order, not to force me to go farther into the subject.
>
> I again reiterate that *every atom* of the knowledge of the Order has come *through me alone* from 0–0 to 5–6 inclusive, and that it is I alone who have been and am in communication with the Secret Chiefs of the Order.[12]

The effect was catastrophic, for Mathers was undermining the very fabric of the Order. The members demanded proof but Mathers, who was clearly becoming deranged, refused to give it and said that he obeyed no one save the Chiefs of the Third Order, adding dark hints that he would request those Chiefs to set in motion the 'deadly and hostile current of will', by which the rebellious members would 'fall slain or paralyzed without visible weapon, as if blasted by the lightning flash'.

His threats, however, were of no avail and seeing both the Outer Order and the R.R. et A.C. at risk, the members deposed Mathers, suspended all Order work and set up a committee, comprising M. W. Blackden, Percy Bullock, Florence Farr, E. A. Hunter and his wife, G. C. Jones and W. B. Yeats, to investigate the allegations about the Anna Sprengel letters. Westcott denied the story and Mathers, sensing the way the tide was running, did not wait for the committee to report but acted at once.

In 1900 the Vault of the Adepts was at 36 Blythe Road, Hammersmith, and Mathers determined to possess it—by force if necessary—and to demand the submission of the rebels. As his instrument he chose Frater Perdurabo, who had taken Mathers' side because Mathers had been prepared to give him his 5 = 6 initiation in Paris after the officers of Isis-Urania refused to advance him to the Second Order because of his sexual peculiarities.

Equally peculiar was his manner of capturing the vault. Under Mathers' instructions Crowley went to Blythe Road, on 17 April 1900, broke into the vault and, in his own words, 'recaptured it'. The occupation was brief for on the 18th, Yeats and Hunter, armed with a letter from Florence Farr, the official tenant, arrived at Blythe Road, gained the landlord's consent and changed the locks. Then 'At about 11.30 Aleister Crowley arrived in Highland dress, a black mask over his face, and a plaid thrown over his head and shoulders, an enormous gold or gilt cross on his breast, and a dagger at his side.'[13] He entered the premises but the landlord called the police and Crowley was ejected, 'saying he should place the matter in the hands of a lawyer'.

No legal action followed. Mathers had lost the fight and his hold on Isis-Urania. On 27 April W. B. Yeats was elected Imperator and a troubled peace descended on the Golden Dawn. It was to be short lived.

Later in 1900 Westcott joined Berridge in the rival Isis-Urania Temple that he ran under Mathers' obedience and became its Praemonstrator. Evidently, he was more forgiving than Mathers or else inclined to believe after all in the Secret Chiefs he had helped to create. While he lay low in Notting Hill the Golden Dawn was receiving unwelcome attention from the public.

Early in the same year Mathers had been approached in Paris by a strange couple who went under the name of Horos, but whose real name was Jackson. They were adventurers and confidence tricksters who were well aware of the ease with which occult pretensions enabled one to part the gullible from their money. To Mathers they announced themselves as High Adepts, Mrs Horos claiming to be the original Anna Sprengel herself. Despite his previous denial of Anna Sprengel's existence, Mathers was taken in and only realized his folly when the two decamped with a mass of Golden Dawn rituals.

They appeared in London in 1901, setting up a bogus occult Order and using it to enable Theo Horos to seduce a succession of young girls. Eventually they were arrested and charged: Theo with rape and Swami Vive Ananda—his wife—with aiding and abetting him. Both were found guilty and they were sentenced to terms of fifteen and seven years imprisonment respectively. None of this would have much mattered had not the trial brought to the public's notice the Neophyte Grade of the Golden Dawn, which had been used by Mr and Mrs Horos in their murky activities. To the horror of the members, the Golden Dawn was held up to ridicule; some, like William Peck in Edinburgh, panicked and destroyed all evidence of their membership; others quietly res-igned and the more determined members set about seeking a new name for the Order in order to dissociate it from the trial. This was not settled until June 1902, when the membership was told that they belonged not to the G.D. but to the M.R., the letters standing for Morgenröthe, the German equivalent of Golden Dawn.

To add to the Order's misery dissension arose among the members over the 'Secret Groups' founded by Florence Farr. These had grown up for the purpose of providing extra-curricular occult activities in the form, principally, of astral travelling. They were harmless enough to the Order but to some members they were anathema. Annie Horniman had returned to the Order after the break with Mathers and was horrified to find the Secret Groups still in evidence; even worse, she found that the system of advancement by examination had fallen into disuse. With the support of W. B. Yeats she tried to have the Groups, or what was left of them, disbanded and the examination system restored, but the membership would have none of it. There followed long and complicated squabbles over the Order's essential nature, involv-ing much pamphleteering and canvassing of support. Dissatisfied with the inconclusive outcome of all this, Annie Horniman, Yeats and Brodie-Innes all resigned from office and the Provisional Council that now governed the Order began to draw up a new Constitution that would effectively remove almost the entire magical element from the Order's teaching and practices.

Nothing came of this and in May 1902 three Chiefs were elected for one year: Percy Bullock, Dr R. W. Felkin and Brodie-Innes (who was unhappy with the prospect of an annual election—he believed that Chiefs should be appointed for life). Felkin had come to London in 1896 from Edinburgh, where he had qualified, although not in the same college, both as a medical and a magical practitioner, and he owed his success in the Order to his conviction that he was in direct contact with the Third Order Chiefs and to his ability to persuade others in the Order of the fact.

Further arguments arose between the Three Chiefs on the one hand and Annie Horniman on the other, ending with her depar-ture from the Order for good. A constitution had still not been approved and another attempt was made in May 1903 to have a further draft constitution accepted by the members. This would, had it been passed, have resulted in Brodie-Innes becoming the effective, autocratic head of the Order; that he failed in his attempt was due entirely to A. E. Waite, who had been preparing the ground in secret for well over a year and who ensured that a large minority rejected the new proposals. For once, his description of events is accurate:

> At the end of twelve months there was a third General Meeting, at which Brodie-Innes declaimed the successive clauses of his Constitution with histrionic magnificence. It fell upon myself subsequently to take the clauses successively, reciting objections and securing promises of variations or amendments in several cases. It began to look ominously as if the draft might pass, subsequent to alteration there and here, and that Brodie-Innes would be claiming the Headship of the Rite in consequence. I proposed therefore the rejection of the second draft Constitution *in toto*, with the result that this also lapsed for want of the requisite majority. It being resolved otherwise that the triumvirate as such should not be elected for a third year, I proposed also that those who regarded the Golden Dawn as capable of mystical instead of an occult construction should and had indeed resolved to work independently, going their own way. This third Annual Meeting dissolved in chaos, so far as other matters were concerned, with Brodie-Innes in a state of white rage.[14]

Not only the meeting but the whole Order had been dissolved. In the form it had taken since 1888 the Golden Dawn was no more.

References:

1   W. B. Yeats, *Memoirs* (1972), p. 27.
2   Arthur Machen, *Things Near and Far* (1923), p. 154.
3   Ellic Howe, *Magicians of the Golden Dawn* (1972), p. 93.
4   A. E. Waite, *Shadows of Life and Thought* (1938), p. 161.
5   Israel Regardie, *The Golden Dawn*, Volume 2 (1938), pp. 155–244.
6   Howe, *op. cit.*, p. 129.
7   [E. Berridge], 'The Rosicrucian Mystery from the Standpoint of a Rosicrucian', in A. E. Waite (ed.), *The Unknown World*, Vol. 1, No. 2 (September 1894), p. 86.
8   Waite, *op. cit.*, p. 126.
9   Howe, *op. cit.*, p. 165.
10 [Aleister Crowley], *The Rosicrucian Scandal*, by Leo Vincey (1913), p. 9.

11 Howe, *op. cit.*, p. 180.
12 ibid., p. 210.
13 ibid., p. 225.
14 Waite, *op. cit.*, p. 228.

4. Wisdom

By the end of 1897 exactly 323 aspiring magicians had been initiated in the various Temples of the Golden Dawn, 97 of whom stayed the course and entered the Second Order. As the Second Order Roll shows a grand total of 120 admissions up to 1902 it seems probable that no more than 400 people entered the Order before the schism of 1903. Many of these soon fell by the wayside and most of those who remained have the fact of their membership as their only claim upon posterity. But some of the members were more interesting; some were lesser literary and artistic figures, numbers of them achieved fame or notoriety in the occult world, a few were scientists. And there was W. B. Yeats.

Yeats was initiated at Mina Mathers' studio on 7 March 1890, when he took the motto 'Demon est Deus Inversus' (The Devil is the converse of God), and was entered as Number 78 on the Outer Order Roll. He was already deeply immersed in the occult, having helped to found the Hermetic Society in Dublin in 1885 and joining the Esoteric Section of the Theosophical Society in 1888. Eastern Theosophy, however, held little for him at this time and he was ever suspicious of Madame Blavatsky's Mahatmas; his real interests are evident in his first contribution to *Lucifer*, 'Irish Fairies Ghosts and Witches', in the introduction to which he reveals his familiarity with Paracelsus and with the doctrine of Elementals. Perhaps it was an Elemental who led Yeats to Mathers, but it was certainly Mathers who brought him into the Golden Dawn, and Yeats freely acknowledged his debt: 'It was through him mainly that I began certain studies and experiences, that were to convince me that images well up before the mind's eye from a deeper source than conscious or subconscious memory.'[1] And through him also Yeats gained his understanding of magic:

> The evoker of spirits and his beautiful wife received us in a little house, on the edge of some kind of garden or park belonging to an eccentric rich man, whose curiosities he arranged and dusted, and he made his evocation in a long room that had a raised place on the floor at one end, a kind of dais, but was furnished meagrely and cheaply. I sat with my acquaintance in the middle of the room, and the evoker of spirits on the dais, and his wife between us and him. He held a wooden mace in his hand, and turning to a tablet of many-coloured squares, with a number on each of the squares, that stood near him on a chair, he repeated a form of words. Almost at once my imagination began to move of itself and to bring before me vivid images that, though never too vivid to be imagination, as I had always understood it, had yet a motion of their own, a life I could not change or shape. I remember seeing a number of white figures, and wondering whether their mitred heads had been suggested by the mitred head of the mace, and then, of a sudden, the image of my acquaintance in the midst of them. I told what I had seen, and the evoker of spirits cried in a deep voice, 'Let him be blotted out', and as he said it the image of my acquaintance vanished, and the evoker of spirits or his wife saw a man dressed in black with a curious square cap standing among the white figures.[2]

The experiment carried on and magic became real for Yeats.

In January 1893 Yeats was initiated into the Second Order, albeit in an unusual manner, for he took the Portal Ceremony and the first part of the Adeptus Minor ritual one Friday and completed the Second and Third points on the day following. Throughout that year Yeats made frequent visits to the vault, initially to consecrate his magical instruments and later, perhaps, to consecrate talismans, carry out magical evocations or to indulge in automatic writing. As a sound disciple of Mathers, Yeats saw the need to treat the Golden Dawn system as a whole and he favoured the system of examinations that ensured a thorough grounding in practical occultism for the newborn magician. Indeed, the pamphlet, *Is the Order of R.R. et A.C. to remain a Magical Order?*,[3] that he issued during his period as Imperator of

Isis-Urania was designed to combat the Groups championed by
Florence Farr and to defend the use of examinations prior to
entry into the grade of Theoricus Adeptus Minor. In it Yeats sees
the Golden Dawn as a living entity:

> Because a Magical Order differs from a society for experiment and
> research in that it is an Actual Being, an organic life holding within
> itself the highest life of its members now and in past times, to weaken
> its Degrees is to loosen the structure, to dislimn, to disembody, to
> dematerialize an Actual Being; and to sever the link between one
> Degree and another, above all between the Degrees that are in the
> Heart, in the Tiphereth, in the $5 = 6$, is to cut this being in two, and to
> confine the magical life of its visible Adepti to the lower substances of
> this being. To do this last thing is to create an evil symbol, to make the
> most evil of all symbols, to awake the energy of an evil sorcery. On the
> other hand, to create within this order, within this Actual Being
> formal 'groups', centres of astral activity, which are not the Degrees of
> this Order, the organs of this Being, is to create centres of life, which
> are centres of death, to this greater life; astral diseases sapping up, as
> it were, its vital fluids.[4]

   This impassioned plea fell upon deaf ears and, as we have seen,
Yeats resigned as Imperator. Later he took the magical side
against Waite and his company in 1903 and became a member of
the Stella Matutina, remaining active until the 1920s. But however
deeply impressed with magic, Yeats never let it overcome his
humanity and he remained sensitive to the views of others,
keeping his friendship with Mina Mathers and corresponding
amicably with Waite and his faction. Most of his fellow magicians
tended to be much less amiable.
   In the preface to *A Vision* Yeats refers, without naming him, to
the artist W. T. Horton who 'was my close friend, and had he lived
I would have asked him to accept the dedication of a book I could
not expect him to approve'. The approval would have been
lacking because Horton had come to dislike magical practices and
Yeats' involvement with them. William Thomas Horton was a
visionary and mystic, manifestly unsuited to the Golden Dawn, in
which he never progressed beyond the Neophyte Grade, but his
brief membership, from March to May of 1896, entitles him to the
doubtful honour of being the only artist of distinction, albeit little
distinction, to enter the Order.
   His work is preserved in *A Book of Images* (1898) and in *The Way*

of the Soul (1910), while at least one of his visions is recorded in an article, *The Legend of Life*, that appeared in *The Occult Review* for December 1912. This is a parable of the quest of a man for his soul, called throughout his Beloved, which is also an analogue of an earthly Platonic union, such as that maintained by Horton and Audrey Locke, the 'very good, charming and young fellow-student' with whom he fell in love late in his life. Such a union was in keeping with the odd sexual-pneumatic philosophy, and even odder practices, of The Brotherhood of the New Life, a movement founded in the late nineteenth century by the occult theorist Thomas Lake Harris, and of which Horton was a disciple. After he left the Golden Dawn Horton joined Papus' Martinist Order and wrote for its journal, *I.N.R.I.*; several members of the Golden Dawn were also active in Martinism, which had a quite compatible philosophy founded on the ideas of Louis Claude de Saint-Martin, and it is difficult to see why the occult ideas of Papus (Gérard Encausse) should have been acceptable to Horton while those of Mathers were not. Later in his life he was involved with yet another obscure society and sought advice about it from A. E. Waite; in the surviving correspondence the name does not appear although it is clear, from the context, that the society was of a highly mystical nature. Horton died in 1919 at the age of 55, reconciled to the Catholic Church but unreconciled either to Yeats or to his Golden Dawn. Yeats remained alive to Horton's reproaches, writing of him in 1925: 'I remember the mystical painter Horton, whose work had little of his personal charm and real strangeness, writing me these words, "I met your beloved in Russell Square, and she was weeping", by which he meant that he had seen a vision of my neglected soul.'[5]

Other members, too, were closely linked to Yeats, the closest and by far the most complex being Florence Farr. She was already established as an actress and knew Yeats as a neighbour and friend at Bedford Park, where she lived under her married name of Emery, before she joined the Order in July 1890. Her enthusiasm for the occult was great and her progress accordingly rapid, her initiation into the Second Order taking place in August 1891. During the period of her membership Soror Sapientia Sapienti Dono Data (Wisdom is given to the wise as a gift) treated the affairs of the Order, and her own occult studies, as far more important than her professional career upon the stage—although not, perhaps, as more important than her affair with George

Bernard Shaw, even though he remained constantly irritated by her preoccupation with magic. Florence's enthusiasm led her to become Praemonstratrix of the Isis-Urania Temple in 1894 and, later, to set up a small study circle for the practice of astral travelling. This circle was seen by Annie Horniman as a threat to the unity of the Order and in 1902 she appealed to the Chiefs of the Second Order to permit her to disperse the group by means of a banishing ceremony, for she believed that there were occult as well as disciplinary reasons for its undesirability. Her petition to the Chiefs describes the group: 'This group consisted of 12 members and the symbols were adapted from the Star maps and Tree of Life projected on a sphere, whence they were sometimes called the sphere group. The twelve members had astral stations assigned to them around this sphere and a certain Egyptian astral form was supposed to occupy the centre.'[6] A paper on the group by Dr Felkin enlarges on its activities and provides us with Florence's justification: 'When the first group was formed by Mrs Emery she told us that D.D.C.F. approved of such groups, as also did S.A. and that indeed S.A. had once formed such a group himself. The objects of the Group were: to concentrate forces of growth, progress and purification, every Sunday at noon, and the progress was 1st, the formulation of the twelve workers near but not in 36; 2nd Formulation round London; 3rd, Formulation round the Earth; 4th, Formulation among the Constellations. Then gradually reverse the process, bringing the quintessence of the greater forces to the lesser. The process was to take about an hour.'[7] The group had disbanded by 1901 so it seems that Annie Horniman's banishing ceremony was to little avail, if it ever took place.

Florence also believed in propagating Hermetic beliefs, and once she had assimilated the teachings of the Second Order (her transcription of *The Book of the Concourse of the Forces*, which contains the essence of Enochian Magic, Egyptian symblolism and astral travelling, was completed, with extra notes, on 12 October 1893) she was eager to give her knowledge to the world. This she did through the medium of Westcott's *Collectanea Hermetica* series, in which she edited Thomas Vaughan's *Euphrates*, annotated *The Hermetic Art* and wrote *Egyptian Magic*. The introduction to *The Hermetic Art* contains this sketch of the true alchemist:

I can hold out no hope of success to those who still retain an absorbing interest in the world. *In* the world Adepts may be, but not *of* it. Alchemy is a jealous mistress, she demands from pupils no less than life; for her sake you must perform the twelve labours of Hercules; for her you must descend into Hell, for her sake you must ascend into Heaven. You must have strength and patience, nothing must terrify you, the joys of Nirvana must not tempt you; having chosen your work, you must to this end purify yourself from perishable desires, and bring down the light of the shining ones, that it may radiate upon you here on earth. This is the work of the Alchemist.[8]

Her own life hardly matched this selfless devotion, but she maintained her enthusiasms in one form or another long after she had left the Golden Dawn behind her and acted out her more significant part in life as a 'New Woman'.

While Florence Farr came into the Golden Dawn through the accident of physical proximity to existing members, Isabelle de Steiger entered it because her own esoteric thinking ran so close to that of its founders. From 1875 she had been an active Spiritualist, by 1880 she was a Theosophist, and then she espoused the Christian Hermeticism of Anna Kingsford, writing regularly for their journals and producing portrait sketches and paintings of the principal figures of each movement as she passed through it.

All this, however, was not enough and she became the 'sole friend and spiritual confidant' of Mrs Atwood, absorbing both that strange woman's zeal for spiritual alchemy and her even stranger interpretation of it. Ultimately, as her literary executor, she succeeded in arranging for the re-publication in 1918 of Mrs Atwood's *Suggestive Enquiry into the Hermetic Mystery*, an event that brought doubtful comfort to all those Hermetic students who had so eagerly desired it. The thesis of the book is, more or less, that the goal of alchemy was to attain a form of exalted mesmeric trance through which enlightenment can come upon one. It ought to have inspired the people of the Golden Dawn but they seem to have found it as confusing as Mme. de Steiger's own works, *On a Gold Basis* and *Superhumanity*, which were both in a similar vein.

Isabelle de Steiger joined the Golden Dawn in October 1888, taking the motto Alta Peto (I strive for the heights), but she did not reach the Second Order until 1895, by which time she had transferred from Isis-Urania to the Amen-Ra Temple in Edinburgh. Here, in addition to painting the 'artistic part of the vault' for the Second Order, she discoursed to Scottish Theosophists on the *Stromata* of Clemens Alexandrinus, and on Regeneration, by which term she meant an esoteric form of Christian redemption. Since many of the members of the Scottish Lodge of the Theosophical Society were also members of the Amen-Ra Temple, the paper was probably heard with less hostility than might have been expected from a Theosophical audience faced with a lecture on the superiority of Christianity over its rivals. Her fellow magicians doubtless appreciated the reference to Mystery Schools: 'There, however, was one great secret and sacred Lodge, an Inner Circle, in possession of the great secrets of human generation and human regeneration; something, though far in degree, different from our notions of an inner circle. It was from this source that the final Consummation of the new dispensation was proclaimed. From the Quabbala [sic], the Essene Brotherhood, and on to the present time, there are glimpses given us, which tell us of the Work that Sacred Lodge performed. Its secrets still survive, and esoteric Christians see unequivocal proofs that the Church of Christendom is the direct successor'.[9]

During the same period she provided A. E. Waite with a series of singularly uninspiring illustrations for his journal *The Unknown World*, compensating for them by her translation of Eckartshausen's *Cloud upon the Sanctuary*, which was published in 1896 with a preface by J. W. Brodie-Innes. Unknown to herself, translating Eckartshausen was the single most significant act of her occult life, for this was the book used by A. E. Waite to persuade Aleister Crowley to take the path that led to the Golden Dawn. In due course Mme. de Steiger joined the rebellion against Mathers, and thus against Crowley, and in 1903 sided with Waite's mystical party. She did not, however, pass on into the Fellowship of the Rosy Cross, for she was lured away by the glamour of Rudolf Steiner—a fate to be suffered in time by other and more important members.

The President of the Scottish Lodge of the Theosophical Society was also the Imperator of the Amen-Ra Temple under his motto of Sub Spe (Under hope). In the real world he was John William Brodie-Innes, an Edinburgh lawyer who joined the Golden Dawn in 1891, bringing with him not only a solid masonic and theosophical background, but a good deal of real learning. Within the Order he was a firm believer in the Secret Chiefs and an ardent supporter of Mathers until 1897, when Mathers deposed him and took the post of Imperator of Amen-Ra upon himself (according to Westcott; it seems more probable that Brodie-Innes was forced to resign in favour of William Peck). After Mathers' deposition and expulsion from the Order in 1900, Brodie-Innes was unhappy with the executive who succeeded him and circulated a pamphlet among the members urging the need for a new constitution and a properly elected Council.

Despite its plea for democracy it is clear that the pamphlet was intended to gain support for Brodie-Innes. It also reiterates his own beliefs: 'I do not forget that ours is an occult and magical Order, and I for one firmly believe in the guidance and supervision of higher powers (whether you call them the Third Order or by any other title), and I believe that such higher powers will take care that all that is worth preserving in the Order as we know it will be preserved.'[10] Whether with supernatural aid or not, Brodie-Innes did become a Chief of the Order in 1902 but his term of office was, as we have seen, short lived.

For all that he was a public figure Brodie-Innes made no secret of his interests and never allowed the problems of the Order to upset his professional life. Witchcraft had always fascinated him and in the course of a lecture on *Scottish Witchcraft Trials*, given in 1891 to a bibliographical society known as The Sette of Odd Volumes, he publicly expressed his belief in supernatural beings. Having argued that hypnosis, auto-hypnosis and hysteria could account for much of so-called witchcraft, he added: 'Of course this is far from accounting for the whole range of phenomena; indeed, unless we accept the theory of the operation of intelligent powers superior to man, some better and some worse, of an intermediary character, neither wholly good nor wholly evil, it is hard to see how observed phenomena can be accounted for with logical completeness, either today or in the sixteenth century.' Later, in the years before the Great War, he wrote a series of historical novels on witchcraft, but it was neither by supernatural influence nor by their intrinsic merit that they were published; more simply it was due to Hugh Elliott, who owned the publishing house of Rebman and Co., being a fellow initiate in the Golden Dawn.

Brodie-Innes' successor as Imperator in Amen-Ra was less open about his occult pursuits. William Peck was the City

Astronomer for Edinburgh, a believer in astrology, a Freemason, Theosophist and a member of Papus' Martinist Order. In the opinion of Mme. de Steiger, Peck was 'a *born* occultist ... a first-rate astronomer and astrologer and accustomed to great thoughts', but he was extremely coy about publicizing his interests. Even his quite objective lectures on astronomy to the Scottish Lodge of the Theosophical Society were published anonymously. He joined the Amen-Ra Temple in 1893, entering the Second Order early in 1895. After Brodie-Innes broke with Mathers, Peck became Imperator but was soon faced with dissension in the ranks from supporters of Brodie-Innes; each side mustered about fifteen Second Order Adepti but Peck was faced with a number of resignations. He could yet count on at least two loyal supporters—his wife and daughter who had followed him eagerly into Amen-Ra.

Problems within the Order Peck could face, but not trouble from without. When the Horos trial exposed the Golden Dawn to ridicule Peck was terrified that his membership would be made public and he himself become a laughing-stock. Westcott told F. L. Gardner that Peck 'was in a ghastly funk over the Horos affair, and hurriedly burnt all his lectures, letters, jewels, robes, etc.'. He doubtless regretted also his choice of motto—Veritas et Lux: Truth and Light.

Peck was not the only astronomer in the Order: Sydney Klein had a large observatory at Stanmore, but was better known for his masonic researches and for a series of popular works on occultism. Other scientists included the chemist Andrew Aitken of Edinburgh University, and William Crookes, although his stay was brief and he never progressed beyond the grade of Neophyte. Medical practitioners were plentiful, the most intriguing being an American, Miss Kate Sands Staunton. She took the Neophyte Grade at the Ahathoor Temple in 1896 but 'became suddenly insane after having passed Exam for 1 = 10'. The same hand that entered this on the Order Roll also entered the letters M.D. after her name, and one wonders whether they have a less obvious reference.

Just as poor frightened Dr Peck was not the only astronomer, so he was not the only member stricken with fear. W. B. Yeats remembered the Revd W. A. Ayton as 'the most panic-stricken person I have ever known' and discovered that Ayton was apprehensive about every aspect of practical occultism:

[He] took me aside that he might say—'I hope you never invoke spirits—that is a very dangerous thing to do. I am told that even the planetary spirits turn upon us in the end'. I said, 'Have you ever seen an apparition?' 'O, yes, once,' he said. 'I have my alchemical laboratory in a cellar under my house where the Bishop cannot see it. One day I was walking up and down there when I heard another footstep walking up and down beside me. I turned and saw a girl I had been in love with when I was a young man, but she died long ago. She wanted me to kiss her. O no, I would not do that.' 'Why not?' I said. 'O she might have got power over me.' 'Has your alchemical research had any success?' I said. 'Yes, I once made the elixir of life. A French alchemist said it had the right smell and the right colour' (the alchemist may have been Eliphas Lévi, who visited England in the 'sixties, and would have said anything) 'but the first effect of the elixir is that your nails fall out and your hair falls off. I was afraid that I might have made a mistake and that nothing else might happen, so I put it away on a shelf. I meant to drink it when I was an old man, but when I got it down the other day it had all dried up.'[11]

Ayton and his wife were among the first to join the Golden Dawn and he was also the oldest member, being 72 when he was initiated in July 1888. He brought with him an impeccable Masonic pedigree, a mania for alchemy and an absolute conviction that England in general and the Golden Dawn in particular were under occult attack by the Jesuits. He was also among the first to enter the Second Order and it was in view of this seniority that he became a Chief of the Order, together with Waite and Blackden, at the time of the schism in 1903.

William Alexander Ayton, when in the guise of Frater Virtute Orta Occident Rarius (Those that rise by virtue rarely fall), was fascinated by Enochian Magic and evocations—in 1908 he translated Thomas Smith's Latin *Life of John Dee*—but always sought to relate them to alchemy, which he pursued to the end, first at Chacombe in Northamptonshire, then at East Grinstead and finally at Saffron Walden, to where he had retired. He transcribed large numbers of alchemical texts and many Golden Dawn papers that would not otherwise have survived. With the latter he was somewhat indiscreet, sending the 5 = 6 ritual, and perhaps other documents, to his fellow alchemist Julius Kohn, who was never a member of the Order and had no business examining the papers. Ayton's indiscretions were of little significance, however, for his influence on the Order and its affairs was minimal, in contrast to his influence upon the modern revival of practical alchemy, which was immense and which has yet to be fully appreciated.

The third of the 1903 triumvirate, with Ayton and Waite, was Marcus Worsley Blackden, a gentleman Egyptologist who joined the Golden Dawn in August 1896, shortly after Waite's re-admission. Unlike Waite, Blackden joined Florence Farr's sphere group, but he and Waite both decided that Masonic initiation was essential for Adepts and accordingly they were both made Masons in 1901. In the following year they both joined the S.R.I.A. and in 1903 they seized the Golden Dawn, although Blackden's active involvement in the new Order was brief, for Waite records that in 1904 Frater Mawahanu Thesi (a supposed and quite untranslatable Egyptian motto) 'married a first cousin and retired to a country house in the neighbourhood of the New Forest'. From there he returned in 1914 to argue against Waite that the cipher rituals could be genuine, having come to the strange belief that the Egyptian fellahin had preserved the hiero-glyphic language to the present day and could thus have trans-mitted ancient and authentic ritual texts.

His re-emergence led to the closing down of the Isis-Urania Temple and Waite's withdrawal of his own rituals from use. Blackden retaliated by producing *The Ritual of the Mystery of the Judgment of the Soul*, a translation from the Papyrus of Ani 'restored to something very like its original form' with the rubrics and commentary supplied by Blackden himself. He saw this ceremony as 'the final gateway into that degree of Initiation, where the traditional Esoteric Wisdom of Egypt was taught and its methods practised by the Initiate'. Many years later Waite met Blackden while walking on the Sussex Downs; he did not record their conversation, but it is safe to assume that whatever else they talked about, they said nothing of the Hermetic Order of the Golden Dawn.

References:
1. W. B. Yeats, *The Trembling of the Veil* (1922), p. 69.
2. W. B. Yeats, *Essays* (1924), pp. 35–36. This essay, 'Magic', was first published in 1901.
3. The text of the pamphlet, and of its Supplement, is published in full in George Mills Harper, *Yeats's Golden Dawn* (1974).
4. [W. B. Yeats] *Is the Order of R.R. et A.C. to Remain a Magical Order?* (1901), pp. 11–12.

5.   W. B. Yeats, *Early Poems and Stories* (1925), p. 527.
6.   Quoted in Ellic Howe, *The Magicians of the Golden Dawn* (1972), p. 247.
7.   ibid., p. 250.
8.   *A Short Enquiry concerning the Hermetic Art, by A Lover of Philalethes* An Introduction to Alchemy and Notes by S.S.D.D. [Florence Farr] (1894), p. 13.
9.   *Transactions of the Scottish Lodge of the Theosophical Society*, Volume II Part 19, p. 143.
10. [J. W. Brodie Innes] *Concerning the Revisal of the Constitution and Rules of the Order R.R. & A.C.* (1901), p. 11.
11. W. B. Yeats, *The Trembling of the Veil* (1922), p. 70.

5. Power

Every member of the Golden Dawn studied both practical and theoretical occultism, but it was often unclear to outsiders just what their studies were. In 1898 Arthur Conan Doyle was asked by Dr Henry Pullen Bury, Frater Anima Pura Sit within the Golden Dawn, to join the Order; later, he recalled the curious conversation that ensued:

Finding that I was interested in such subjects, Dr Bury suggested one day that I should join a secret society of esoteric students. The invitation had been led up to by a good deal of preparatory inquiry. The dialogue between us ran somewhat thus: – 'What shall I get from it?'

'In time, you will get powers.'

'What sort of powers?'

'They are powers which people would call supernatural. They are perfectly natural, but they are got by knowledge of deeper forces of nature.'

'If they are good, why should not everyone know them?'

'They would be capable of great abuse in the wrong hands.'

'How can you prevent their getting into wrong hands?'

'By carefully examining our initiates.'

'Should I be examined?'

'Certainly.'

'By whom?'

'The people would be in London.'

'Should I have to present myself?'

'No, no, they would do it without your knowledge.'

'And after that?'

'You would then have to study.'

'Study what?'

'You would have to learn by heart a considerable mass of material. That would be the first thing.'

'If this material is in print, why does it not become public property?'

'It is not in print. It is in manuscript. Each manuscript is carefully numbered and trusted to the honour of a passed initiate. We have never had a case of one going wrong.'

'Well,' said I, 'it is very interesting, and you can go ahead with the next step, whatever it may be.'[1]

The 'next step' was an astral examination of Conan Doyle, which he found 'queer and disagreeable' and he declined to join, although he became convinced that Pullen Bury was clairvoyant, at the least, and that there was more to the Order than met the eye: 'I remain under the impression that I brushed against something strange, and something which I am not sorry that I avoided. It was not Spiritualism and it was not Theosophy, but rather the acquisition of powers latent in the human organization, after the alleged fashion of the old gnostics or of some modern fakirs in India, though some, doubtless, would spell fakirs with an "e".'[2]

But the Secret Chiefs were not fakers. Westcott was a firm believer in occult forces and Mathers was a fully fledged ritual magician; it is most unlikely that any member who remained in the Golden Dawn, and certainly none who entered the Second Order, were not fully convinced that what they learned there concerned a reality: beyond Nature, but a reality nonetheless. Their progress in occultism and magic depended on such a belief.

In the First Order that progress was by means of examinations into the student's divinatory ability and knowledge of the Kabbalah, but they did not require much intellectual power. Aleister Crowley was disappointed when he received his first Knowledge Lecture: 'And now I was entrusted with some of these devastating though priceless secrets. They consisted of the Hebrew alphabet, the names of the planets with their attribution to the days of the week, and the ten Sephiroth of the Cabbala. I had known it all for months; and, obviously, any schoolboy in the lower fourth could memorize the whole lecture in twenty-four hours.'[3]

There was, of course, more to it than that. The Hebrew

Kabbalah was seen in the Golden Dawn not so much as it originally was, a mystical interpretation of the Books of the Pentateuch, but as a receptacle of occult wisdom containing a complete interpretation of the Seen and Unseen Universes. During his advancement from Neophyte to Philosophus, the student must learn not only the names, natures and attributions of the ten Sephiroth of the Kabbalistic Tree of Life, but also the twenty-two Paths on the Tree, the correct attribution of the Tarot Trumps to the Hebrew alphabet and the nature and colour correspondences of the Four Worlds of the Kabbalah. He had further to learn about alchemical symbolism, angelic and elemental spirits, Geomancy and Tarot divination, and was required to construct the badge of admission—heavy with symbolism—for each grade as he entered it.

On a more practical level the student learned the Pentagram Ritual. This was used both for invoking Elemental spirits and for banishing them; it was also the nearest thing to a purely magical ritual found within the First Order curriculum. Published rituals of the Order, both Crowley's and Regardie's, give technically accurate versions of the ritual, but a more general description of it was made public (without acknowledging its source) by Dion Fortune:

> In dealing with elementals or non-human entities the Pentagram, or Pentalpha, is the best weapon. This is a five-pointed star drawn in a particular way. Pointing the first and second fingers of the right hand, and folding the others into the palm and touching their tips with the thumb, proceed to draw the Pentagram in the air, keeping the elbow stiff and swinging the arm at full length. Start with the right arm across the body, the hand about the level of the left hip, the extended fingers pointing downwards and outwards. Swing it upwards as if drawing a straight line in the air, until the fingers point straight upwards above the head at arm's length. Now sweep it down again, keeping the elbow stiff, until the hand occupies the corresponding position upon the right side to that from which it started on the left. You have now drawn a gigantic V upside down. Next swing the hand across the body, on a rising incline, until it is stretched on a level with the left shoulder, pointing to the left. Bring it across the body horizontally until it is in the same position on the right, fingers pointing away from the body. Now swing it downwards across the body till the hand has come back to the point by the left hip whence it started. This is an exceedingly potent sign. The value of the Five-

pointed Star, the symbol of Humanity, is widely known among occultists, but its potency depends upon the manner in which it is drawn. The method I have given is the correct one for banishing.[4]

Equally important, but more subjective, was the subject of astral travelling by means of Tattwa vision. The Tattwas are coloured symbols of the elements as used—or as the Golden Dawn occultists *believed* them to be used—by Hindu adepts, who recognized five elements rather than the four accepted in the West. They are: Tejas, a red equilateral triangle; Apas, a horizontal silver crescent; Vayu, a blue circle; Prithivi, a yellow square; and Akasa, a black egg. By superimposing these symbols upon each other in various ways it is possible to obtain thirty different symbols, each of which produces a different type of vision, appropriate to the elements concerned, when used as a focus for occult meditation.

First Order students learned the theory of obtaining clair-voyance through meditation upon these symbols, but astral travelling, or 'Travelling in the Spirit Vision', was confined to the Second Order, whose members were given the theoretical basis as part of 'Ritual U', *The Secret Wisdom of the Lesser World or Microcosm which is Man* (See Appendix E). Such travelling proved immensely popular, but whether used for exploring one's inner self or for projecting images from the Tree of Life, it is a process susceptible to self-deception, although the visions recorded by Second Order members reflect the magical practices they had learned as much, or more, than their own psychological peculiar-ities. The following vision was recorded by Miss Harriet Butler, Soror A Posse ad Esse, who joined the Order in 1895; it is interesting to compare it with the Group vision printed as Appendix F as it was probably experienced about the same time, late in 1900, and Miss Butler seems to have been involved with the same group.

I have tried to gain some knowledge as you suggest and just send you a short result. I followed your path along the symbols named in the paper and saw in thought what you saw until I came to the red river flowing from white light. Up to this point nothing was very distinct, I think I just saw a thought reflection of your vision. At this point a guide came to me—not angelic—a human looking teacher with whom I have been out astrally before. He took my right hand in his left and *my* sword in his right hand held pointing up and forward. Saying to me 'Do not think any more, watch', we passed on, vibrating Elohim Gibor, our feet a little above the red river, it became pale in hue and then nearly white. Then I lost the river but looked into a luminous white fog. After a time there came figures in the fog, coming and going they at last came to me clearly as 7 vast godlike forms, each holding a gigantic sword like my guide pointed up. Then the 7 joined the swords so that the points touched above them. Instantly the white light streamed down but each sword transmitted a different colour, they flowed down past us and behind, a many coloured stream.

Then I heard above us one magnificent tone of sound, it seemed to pass down the 7 swords and became all sounds mingled and clashing together, mostly discordant to me and painful, but sometimes I caught a grand chord. Then my guide held the sword across us so that I took the point in my left hand. The force was intolerable and the pain severe.

I tried with this force to look behind me, I think I wanted to see where the light became white again and the clashing sound pleasant, but I did not. The divided colours flowed behind and were lost to me in a cloud. The sounds were discordant nearly all the time, and the contact of the sword was only intolerable pain except that I seemed to know that if I held on it would cease.

That is all—the vision seems to mean 'Life from unity through division (sword)'. The unity behind which I hoped to see is (I remembered after) not sword symbolism. Please send me any thoughts which any of you gather. I am very pleased if I can join you in this way.[5]

The vision brings to mind the frontispiece of Mathers' book, *The Book of the Sacred Magic of Abra-Melin the Mage* (1898), which was widely known in the Order. This is *real* magic, but Mathers makes clear in the Introduction his own rejection of Black Magic, which he sets in opposition to the Qabalistic Magic that was practised in his Order. He also reiterates his firm belief in the reality and malice of 'such fearful potencies as Amaymon, Egyn and Beelzebub' and the necessity of right preparation: 'Pentacles ar. 1 Symbols are valuable as an equilibrated and fitting basis for the reception of Magical force; but unless the Operator can *really* attract that force to them, they are nothing but so many dead, and to him worthless, diagrams. But used by the initiate who fully comprehends their meaning, they become to him a powerful protection and aid, seconding and focussing the workings of his Will.'[6] In an earlier work, *The Key of Solomon the King* (1889), he warns against the evil use of magic: 'Let him who . . . determines to work evil be assured that this evil will recoil on himself and that he will be struck by the reflex current.' Dion Fortune, however, thought that working any kind of magical, as opposed to initiatory, rituals was always fraught with danger: 'I cannot say much upon these subjects, for they are among the most secret paths of occult lore. Enough must be hinted, however, to reveal what, under certain circumstances, may be experienced. I do not think it in the least likely, however, that the Qlippotic demons will be encountered save through the use of ceremonial magic. They are as rare as anthrax in England, but it is as well to know the manner of their manifestation so that, when encountered, they may be recognized.'[7]

Most magical work in the Second Order did not, however, involve the risk of meeting with demons from the Qlippoth and was a good deal more prosaic. It was concerned with the making and consecration of the Adeptus Minor's magical instruments: the Lotus Wand, lamen, sword and four elemental weapons, which were a wand (fire), a cup (water), a dagger (air), and a pantacle (earth), and which corresponded to the four suits of the Tarot. The instructions for making the instruments are detailed and precise; constructing them was a complicated affair and could be done by none save the adept himself. Speaking of the Lotus Wand, the instructions say: 'It is to be made by himself unassisted, and to be consecrated by himself alone. It is to be untouched by any other person, and kept wrapped in white silk or linen, free from external influences other than his own on the human plane.'

Touching a magical wand could be perilous. Crowley refers in his *Confessions* to an incident involving Allan Bennett; the wand concerned was unusual but the principle was the same: 'He used to carry a "lustre"—a long glass prism with a neck and pointed knob such as adorned old-fashioned chandeliers. He used this as a wand. One day, a party of theosophists were chatting sceptically about the power of the "blasting rod". Allan promptly produced his and blasted one of them. It took fourteen hours to restore the incredulous individual to the use of his mind and his muscles.'[8]

Normally such drama was reserved for the adepts of the Golden Dawn working alone or in a group of fellow members. The Second Order diaries record their activities, which were principally consecrations, divination and invocation. True to the pseudo-Egyptian traditions of the Order the last were frequently taken from Graeco-Egyptian magical papyri which had been translated in the 1850s. The following magical invocation was transcribed by Ayton, who presumably overcame his normal state of panic terror in order to carry it out. I have omitted the ritual directions so that the reader may recite it, if he wishes, in perfect safety:

Thee I invoke the Bornless One
Thee that didst create Earth and Heavens
Thee that didst create Night and Day
Thee that didst create Darkness and Night.
Thou art OSORRONOPHRIS whom no man hath seen at any
*   time*
Thou art IABAS, Thou art IAROS
Thou hast distinguished between the just and the unjust.
Thou didst make the female and the male.
Thou didst produce the seed and the fruit.
Thou didst form men to love one another and to hate one
*   another.*
I AM Moses Thy prophet, unto whom Thou didst commit thy
*   Mysteries, the Ceremonies of Israel.*
Thou didst produce the moist and the dry and that which
*   nourisheth all created life.*
Hear Thou me, for I am the Angel of PAPHRO
*   OSORRONOPHRIS. This is Thy true Name handed down*
*   to the Prophets of Israel.*
Hear me, AR THIAO RHEIBET ATHELEBERSETH A
*   BLATHA AEU EBEN PHI CHITASOE IB THIAO.*
Hear me, and make all Spirits subject unto me, so that every
*   Spirit of the firmament and of Ether: upon the earth and*
*   under the earth, on dry land and in water, of whirling air,*
*   and of rushing fire and every spell and scourge of God may be*
*   obedient unto me!*
I invoke Thee the terrible and invisible God Who dwellest in the
*   void place of the Spirit.*
Hear me AROGOGOROBRAO: SOCHOU MODURIO
*   PHALARCHAO OOÖ APÉ: The Bornless One,*
Hear me and make all Spirits . . . [as above]
Hear me ROUBRAIO: MARIODAM BALNABAOTH
*   ASSALONAI APHNIAO I THOLETH ABRASAX Ä Ē*

*ÖÖÜ ISCHURE. Mighty and Bornless One, Hear me and
make all Spirits . . . [as above]*
*I invoke Thee MA BARRAIO IOEL KOTHA ATHOREBALO
ABRAOTH, Hear me and make etc.*
*Hear me AOTH ABAOTH BASUM ISAK SABAOTH IAO.
This is the Lord of the gods.*
*This is the Lord of the Universe. This is He Whom the winds
fear. This is He who having made Voice by His
commandment, is Lord of all things, King, Ruler and Helper.*
Hear me and make all Spirits subject unto me . . . [as above]
*Hear me IEOU PUR: IOU: PUR: IAOT IAEO IOOU:
ABRASAS SABRIAM OO UU ADONAIE: EDE EDU
ANGELOS TOU THEOU ANLALA IAI GAIA ARA
DIACHAN NA CHORUN.*
*I am the Bornless Spirit: Light in the feet, strong and the
immortal fire.*
I am the Truth.
I am He who hateth that evil should be wrought in the World.
I am He that lighteneth & thundereth.
I am He from whom is the shower of the life of the Earth.
I am He whose mouth ever flameth.
I am He the begetter & manifester unto Light.
I am the Grace of the World.
The heart girt with a serpent is My Name.
*Come thou forth & follow me and make all Spirits subject unto
me . . . [as above]*
*I invoke Thee, terrible and invisible God Who dwellest in the
void place of the Spirit.*
IAO SABAO

Such are the Words.

Ayton was more at home with alchemy than with magic, but he was also a great traveller on the astral planes. Nor was he alone in combining the two. Among Ayton's papers is a short account of the alchemical *Use of the Tablets*. It is unsigned but appears to be in Mathers' hand:

Before commencing any Alchemical process, and at the different stages of it, bring the Cucurbite, Retort, Crucible, or other vessel containing the Matter, place it in the centre of the table and range the

Tablets round it thus: White Tablet with Head (North), Black and Grey Tablet with white pentacle (East), Tablet with Crystal (South), Coloured Tablet with Hexagram (West). (The Operator stands in the South).

Then endeavour according to the directions to see in the Crystal and go to the Alchemical plane corresponding under the Sephira of (Chokmah) where ask the Governor of Hylech to send down the Divine Light into the Matter, the LVX. Perform what other operations you wish and then remove the Tablets and continue the Alchemical processes as usual. In the intervals between the stages etc. act as here prescribed.

Description of the Plane. A beautiful garden in which is a fountain issuing from a pillar and filling a large oblong basin with a certain white water. This place is guarded by an Angel with a Caducean Wand, who represents Metatron on this plane. Ask him to bring you before the Throne of the Governor of Hylech. Above the Pillar is a Globe and the Bird of Hermes human-headed. Further on is the throne of the Governor of Hylech who has rainbow colours about him. There are also near him the 4 Angels of the Elements, the Red King and White Queen etc. and many other symbolic forms. Ask the Governor of Hylech that the Divine LVX may be sent into the Matter and give as your symbols (the Pyramid) and (the Rose Cross).

Alchemical symbolism and correspondences were learned in the First Order, but in the Second Order practical alchemy was pursued by those who desired it—Ayton especially, but Percy Bullock and Florence Farr were also enthusiasts. Mathers endeavoured to keep in their minds the association of alchemy with Enochian magic, and placed this exhortation as a Foreword to a transcription of the *Aurea Catena Homeri*, an alchemical text of the eighteenth-century by Anton Kirchweger that was circulated among some of the members:

Note by GH. Fra. D.D.C.F. ⑦ = 4 —concerning this M.S. of the 'Aurea Catena Homeri'. Let not the Adept, who upon the perusal of this, wishes to put into practice any experiments, forget the importance of the use of Invocations and Flashing Tablets, seeing that without their employment in Alchemy, no truly great result can be arrived at; and that the constant practice of the *Material without the Higher*, will gradually lead the Alchemist farther and farther from Divine Magic, until at length he will become a mere blinded practitioner of the Hermetic Mysteries, and little if any better than the ordinary so-called Scientist.

Wherefore I earnestly recommend that this M.S. be only circulated among those Adepts who have studied that portion of the 'Book of the Voice of (Thoth)', which is called 'The Enterer of the Threshold'. D.D.C.F. ⑦ = 4 .

Unlike the First Order, in which an understanding of the Kabbalah was the foundation on which other studies were built, the true foundation of the Second Order was Enochian Magic. This was derived from the crystal-gazing activities of the Elizabethan polymath and occultist Dr John Dee and his devious skryer, Edward Kelley. They claimed—or, at least Kelley did, for Dr Dee could not see or hear the spirits—that the Angels they saw in the crystal spoke to them in an unknown language which they called Enochian. The Angels further gave them the Enochian alphabet of twenty-one letters, and a series of large tablets subdivided to produce 49 × 49 smaller squares each containing an Enochian letter. From these Dee and Kelley were taught to extract and to translate the nineteen Enochian Keys or Calls, which were magical invocations. Certain of the tablets, called the Four Watchtowers, were to be arranged into elemental squares— the Great Eastern Quadrangle of Air, the Great Western Quadrangle of Water, the Great Northern Quadrangle of Earth and the Great Southern Quadrangle of Fire—with a central Tablet of Union referred to the Spirit. The use of these Tablets and Keys is extremely complex and Second Order adepts were given detailed instruction as to their construction, correct colouring, use and correspondences in Manuscript S, *The Book of the Concourse of the Forces*. It explains why the Enochian language is so important: 'These special Angelical Language letters have more magical virtue than the common Hebrew, or English letters; especially in respect to the working of the squares of the Tablets in Spirit vision or the so called method of skrying in the spirit vision: they are therefore more sigils than simply letters.' A modified form of the whole text is printed in Regardie's final volume.

A later manuscript, labelled 'Y', explains the occult significance of the game of chess, and gives the basis of one of Mathers' most fascinating inventions—Enochian chess. According to Mathers, 'like the Tarot originals the chess pieces were anciently small figures of Egyptian Gods, representing the operation of the Divine forces of nature'. They were thus ideal for transference to the Enochian Tablets, where they represent 'the motion of the ruling angels over the servient Squares'. The moves of the pieces are complicated, being possible in three dimensions rather than two, and it is unlikely that the adepts played Enochian chess purely as a pastime. Nor was the Tarot treated frivolously.

The teaching of Tarot symbolism and divination through the Tarot began in the Neophyte Grade, but this teaching was not original, having been taken from the dreams of Eliphas Lévi, who was the first to make the connection between the twenty-two Tarot Trumps and the twenty-two letters of the Hebrew alphabet. Such a correspondence was a delight to the Kabbalists of the Golden Dawn, who propagated the principle of this newborn 'Ancient Wisdom' with all the zeal of converts, although they altered the sequence of the cards and thus of their particular attributions. The reversal of cards 8 and 11, Strength and Justice, has frequently been blamed on A. E. Waite, who was the first to publish such an attribution, but he took it from the original '3 = 8 Grade of Practicus Side Lecture No. 2', *On the Tarot Trumps*, which was the work of Mathers himself. Other members concerned themselves with relating the four suits of the Tarot to the Four Worlds of the Kabbalah. The resulting wealth of correspondences between the Minor Arcana, planetary symbols and the ten Sephiroth was entered, together with the meanings of the cards, on large cards which were then used for instructional purposes.

There was, in theory, no end to the speculation and magical activity open to the Adepts of the Golden Dawn, but human memory has its limits (the Secret Chiefs never turned their minds to devising a mnemonic system) and the human lifespan is finite. Even magic has its bounds.

References:
1. A. Conan Doyle, 'Early Psychic Experiences', in *Pearson's Magazine* (March 1924), pp. 208–209.
2. ibid., p. 209.
3. Aleister Crowley, *The Confessions* (1969), p. 177.
4. Dion Fortune, *Psychic Self-Defence* (1935), p. 189.
5. Contained in a letter from 'A Posse ad Esse' (Harriet Butler) to an un-named Soror. The letter is sent from the Esmond Hotel, Montague Street, Russell Square, where Miss Butler lived.
6. S. L. M. Mathers, op. cit., pp. xxxvi–xxxvii.
7. Dion Fortune, *Psychic Self Defence*, p. 97.
8. Aleister Crowley, *The Confessions*, p. 180.

6. Emanation

By 1903 the Golden Dawn, in name at least, was dead, but the scattered fragments lived on, mostly with high-sounding names and low-principled leaders. Following Waite's *coup d'état* of 4 July the opposition was in disarray: attempts at a compromise which would have kept the Order more or less intact came to nothing because the differences between the opposing camps were ultimately irreconcilable.

Waite and his party rejected the autocratic rule of one person and insisted on returning to the system of Three Chiefs, who should all be Freemasons—effectively excluding women from the governance of the Order, although the Manifesto of 24 July[1] states that 'we have no idea of excluding women from membership or from office within the Order, apart from the Masonic Chieftanship'. They also refused to be committed over the question of the existence of a Third Order, they objected 'to the principle of practical examination within the Second Order' and in the First Order objected to 'the continued use of the original defective rituals', which they required to be 're-edited in strict accordance with the cipher manuscripts'.

All this was difficult enough for both Felkin or Brodie-Innes to accept, but worse still was the insistence on throwing out magic lock, stock and barrel. Paragraph 10 of the Manifesto was anathema to the magical adepts: 'We affirm that the earliest status of the Order was mystical and that the trend of the Order practice towards the lower occultism rose with the rise and grew with the

growth of the ascendancy of a single Chief. Attention was
originally paid to the mystic way, more especially when the studies
were chiefly directed by S.A. We desire to give prominence to this
method of progress.'

Despite this, Brodie-Innes corresponded with Waite on the
question of a possible concordat between the two parties, but
irritated him with a series of pointed questions about the Manifesto. Unwilling to concede the rights of any viewpoint save his
own Waite ignored Brodie-Innes' perfectly reasonable requests
for further discussions and brought the correspondence to an
abrupt end in December 1903, having first made the two opposing
positions clear: 'You and I approach our subject from an entirely
different point of view. As my last letter will have explained to you
I regard the Order, at least in its present position, simply as the
custodian of certain knowledge but with its laws and constitutions
and its essentials of government still to be made but you appear to
imply throughout the correspondence that there is already some
constituted authority or teaching voice within it and pray pardon
me if I say that perhaps unconsciously you seem to speak as its
interpreter.' This was both perceptive and prescient—Brodie-
Innes did, indeed, believe in the authority of the Third Order and
of their mouthpiece, MacGregor Mathers, and in due course he
found his way back to Mathers' fold.

On 7 November 1903, the Independent and Rectified Rite held
its first Convocation, at Mark Masons' Hall, and the members
were presented with a Report of the events since June, the
correspondence with Brodie-Innes was displayed and the offer of
a concordat left open, while it was announced that the new Rite
'will act henceforward in all respects as the governing body,
assuming in this capacity the charge of the Outer Order and of the
members thereof'.

Now firmly in charge, for Blackden effectively retired from the
Order upon his marriage in 1904, and Ayton—now known as
Frater Aryabhatha—was too frail to attend meetings, Waite set
about turning the Order away from magic and along the mystical
path. His own 'Historical Notes' on the Order reflect his determination only in an oblique manner:

> In this manner Frater Sacramentum Regis became automatically the
> Chief Adept in charge of the Golden Dawn. The lower Grades of the
> Order had met for years on Saturdays at Mark Masons' Hall, Great

Queen Street, and continued to do so. The Second Order, represented erroneously *ab inceptione* by the 5 = 6 Grade and certain
connected Lectures, met separately at various houses rented for the
purpose and set apart thereto.

There was one at Staple Inn, London, which continued for several
years and another on the outskirts of Kensington, to the North West
of Earl's Terrace, both being prior to the expulsion of a certain Chief.
Subsequent to that event and the foundation of the Order as an
Independent and Rectified Rite, there was a house at Acton, abutting
on Horn Lane, in proximity to the Great Western Railway Station;
but it came to an end with the marriage of Mawahanu Thesi, when the
House of the Second Order was located at Penywern Road, Earl's
Court, in convenient premises for something like ten years. It was
during this prosperous period that Frater Sacramentum Regis, endorsed by the Adepti Minores, relegated the original Rituals of the
Golden Dawn to a place in the Archives and produced others *de novo*,
retaining a certain root in some so-called cipher manuscripts which
constituted the source and warrant whereon the Rite was based. The
fact of their existence, however, was known only to a few.

Waite retained the Outer Order rituals with little change until
1910, when they were heavily revised, or as he put it 'newly
constructed from the cipher manuscripts', and were, for the first
time, issued to members in printed form 'by the authority of the
concealed superiors of the Second Order'. It seems unlikely that
he worked any Second Order rituals other than those for the
'Consecration of a Vault and Temple of the Adepts' and 'The
Pontifical Ceremony of Celebrating the Festival of Corpus
Christi', which he called alternatively 'The Recurrence of the
Summer Solstice'; even these seem to have been abandoned after
1910.

How many members followed Waite and Co. is not known, but
there were fourteen signatories to the Manifesto and a further
fifteen members at the Second Convocation in April 1904. Among
them were Arthur Machen (Frater Avallaunius), who had 'returned by special invitation of the Chiefs', Algernon Blackwood
(Umbra Fugat Veritas) and Pamela Colman Smith (Quod Tibi id
Aliis), whom Waite recognized as a 'draughtswoman among us
who, under proper guidance, could produce a Tarot with an
appeal in the world of art and a suggestion of significance behind
the Symbols which would put on them another construction than
had ever been dreamed by those who, through many generations,

had produced and used them for mere divinatory purposes'.[2] He
also recruited Evelyn Underhill (Quaerens Lucem), who seems
to have joined the Independent Rite in 1905. On 2 December of
that year she took her 3 = 8 degree, having earlier written to Waite
to say: 'I am glad you are inclined to be lenient about the
knowledge lecture: I can manage the Hebrew pretty well, but the
astrology and fortune telling are quite beyond me!' Divination
was evidently allowed to go by the board if necessary.

A Concordat was eventually drawn up between the Independent and Rectified Rite and the Stella Matutina, and duly signed,
in April 1907, by Waite and Felkin; Brodie-Innes sent his agreement to the signing but made it clear that the onus for making it
work was entirely Felkin's: 'After hearing Our Frater Finem
Respice's explanations in regard to the position between the two
sections of the Order of the G.D. I hereby agree to his signing the
Concordat which he has arranged, on the understanding that he
is personally responsible for the same. Sub Spe. Th.A.M.' The
full text of the Concordat has not been preserved but from
extracts in letters it is clear that it gave the Chiefs mutual access to
the Order Rolls and permitted members of each section to talk
freely to members of the other about such rituals as were common
to both. The authority of each section over its own members was
recognized by the other and poaching of members was dis-
allowed—although unsolicited transfers did occur.

All went well until 1910, when Waite discovered that Felkin was
not the sole Chief of his section, despite the fact that in the
Concordat he had stated that the Head of the Stella Matutina was
'the Most Honoured Frater Finem Respice, 7 = 4, and him only'.
Waite wrote to Felkin on 19 July demanding an explanation and
threatening that without a satisfactory reply 'the Concordat
ceases from the date of this letter'. Felkin managed to placate
Waite, but he remained wary until a final break occurred between
Felkin and Brodie-Innes.

He also had troubles brewing within his own section. On the
surface all appeared well; Lorimer Thomson (Nosce Teipsum),
who had left Amen-Ra some years before, joined Waite's Independent Rite in 1908 and was able to say that he felt certain 'that
the order is one where harmony prevails amongst all the members'. But that harmony was disturbed when Waite began to
examine the true nature of the cipher manuscripts. He described
his findings in his 'Historical Notes': 'The researches of Frater

Sacramentum Regis, in communication with the famous Egyptologist Sir Wallis Budge [E.A.], made evident that the alleged ci-
phers, considerable portions of which were written on watermark
paper of 1808, had been so prepared with intent to deceive and
were not only subsequent to the discovery of the Rosetta Stone but
were later than the publication of *Isis Unveiled*.' This, of course,
rendered the cipher manuscripts worthless—a conclusion that
upset many of Waite's more credulous followers. The consequences were disastrous. In 1914, 'a second internecine feud followed, in which Frater Mawahanu Thesi emerged from retire-
ment to maintain, in the absence of all evidence, that the Egyptian
fellaheen, long prior to the discovery in question could have been
and probably were acquainted with the fact that certain hiero-
glyphic texts were Funerary Rituals. After an unprofitable debate
Frater Sacramentum Regis, as Chief Adept in Charge, withdrew
his copyright Rituals and dissolved the Rite as at that time
constituted.' Created by the cipher manuscripts, Isis-Urania had
finally been destroyed by them.

While all this was shaking the foundations of Waite's edifice,
Felkin was busy shoring up his own by hunting for the Secret
Chiefs. In 1903, having lost Isis-Urania to Waite, Felkin set up his
own Amoun Temple in London and carried on the Golden Dawn
workings in more traditional style, with himself as Imperator,
Brodie-Innes in a somewhat shadowy role but a Co-Chief in
effect, and Hugh Elliott (Nobis Est Victoria) as Cancellarius.
Privately Felkin communicated—to his own satisfaction—with
the Secret Chiefs by means of automatic writing, and they
convinced him of the genuineness of the cipher manuscripts and
sent him a new Adeptus Minor ritual. He was also promised new
rituals for the higher Grades of $6 = 5$ and $7 = 4$ by other astral
entities known as the Sun Masters. These were 'the hidden
masters of a Sun Order, still, we are told, in existence, and to
which these chiefs belonged, closely connected with and in-
fluencing the Golden Dawn, and which started in Edinburgh
some time in the early nineties'.[3] Brodie-Innes also was supposed
to have had contact with the Sun Masters but there is no evidence,
except—perhaps—on the astral plane, that there ever was a Sun
Temple in Edinburgh.

On a more mundane level Felkin had the task of persuading his
fellow officers of the Stella Matutina to accept the Concordat with
Waite's Independent and Rectified Rite. Brodie-Innes agreed,

but Elliott, in a letter to Felkin of 26 April 1906, suggested obtaining astral advice: 'I should refer it all to Headquarters', by which he meant the Third Order, who were the only justification for the Amoun Temple's claim to retain the Order Rolls: 'Our real claim to the possession of these rolls is our connection with the 3rd Order. This, of course, we can't bring forward, but the fact remains, *L'Ordre c'est nous.*' Eventually Elliott agreed, but he still advised caution: 'We don't want their members working with us, and we certainly can't confer on them any of our special knowledge, unless they conform to the 3rd Order regulations.'

Felkin now set out to find living Secret Chiefs in the flesh. By chance, he had, in 1904, come across a real Anna Sprengel who had written to him from Germany for his clover-tea tablets, which she thought would help her medically. She made no claim to be related to Soror Sapiens Dominabitur Astris, and Felkin never managed to meet her although he remained convinced that she was a niece of *the* Anna Sprengel.

He did, however, meet up with German Rosicrucians in 1906 when trying to visit Fraulein Sprengel, but they were unwilling to tell him anything because he was not a Mason. This lack he remedied in Edinburgh in the following year and in 1910 he returned to Germany seeking more Rosicrucians and the tomb of Christian Rosenkreuz. He found neither, but he did meet Rudolf Steiner who impressed him greatly, although he later told Waite that Steiner was uncouth and 'might not be liked in England'. As a consequence Anthroposophical teachings (Steiner's variations on the Theosophical theme) rapidly gained prominence amongst the gathered wisdom of the Stella Matutina.

In 1912 Felkin finally gained the initiation he sought: 'In June and July 1912 Frather F. R. and Soror Q. L. (Mrs Felkin) were able to go to Germany, and altogether visited five Rosicrucian Temples in different parts of the Continent, and were initiated themselves, Soror Q.L. obtaining grades equivalent to our $7 = 4$ and Frater F.R. $8 = 3$ . . . The Rituals not being in MS. form they are memorized.'[4] Felkin had known what to expect, for one of his adepts, Neville Meakin (Ex Oriente Lux), had already visited the German Rosicrucians and reported his experiences both to Felkin and to Waite.

During the Summer of 1911 Meakin was initiated in Steiner's 'Rosicrucian' Order, attaining the 3rd degree, which he thought was equivalent to the $5 = 6$ Grade in the Golden Dawn although there were few outward similarities: the German Order officers wore clothing like that of the Masonic Royal Arch and there was neither vault nor pastos. Instead, the candidate was blindfolded and expected to imagine the vault as it existed on the astral plane. Meakin was fortunate, for after a fourteen-hour preparation his initiation took only three hours, whereas it should have taken twenty-six. He was also taught a great deal of occult lore; on his return to England he showed Waite a series of Tarot cards he had made in accordance with the German Order's attributions, which were derived from magical squares of the planets. Waite could identify only three and was unimpressed.

Nor was Brodie-Innes impressed with Felkin's junketings around the Continent. He had returned in 1910 to Mathers' fold by joining Dr Berridge (Resurgam) in his Isis Temple of Alpha and Omega in West London while yet remaining in the Stella Matutina (Felkin learned of this duplicity from Waite). The move may have come about from a revived loyalty to Mathers following his attempt to prevent Crowley from publishing the Golden Dawn rituals in *The Equinox*; all the scattered Temples were alarmed by Crowley's action, having memories of the Horos scandal, but few of them gave Mathers any financial support—even Berridge gave only a small amount while nothing at all came from Isis-Urania.

In addition to joining Isis, Brodie-Innes also refounded the Amen-Ra Temple at Edinburgh in December 1910. At the first meeting twelve people were present, including Brodie-Innes and his wife. The others included Dr and Mrs Carnegie Dickson and Kate Moffat, all of whom were supposedly loyal to Felkin. He, in turn, seems not to have worried unduly as he felt sure that the Dicksons at least would return when they found out Brodie-Innes' real nature, which was that of an unprincipled power-seeker. As long as it was convenient to remain with Felkin he did so, as he did with Mathers, for in 1912 Brodie-Innes was quite prepared to ditch Mathers if Felkin would help him to take over the surviving Golden Dawn Temples.[5]

Felkin, however, was taken up ever more with his recently acquired Arab teacher, Ara Ben Shemesh, and the lunacies streaming out from this astral entity were too much for Brodie-Innes, who broke completely with Felkin and the Stella Matutina. The Order, however, went from strength to strength. After his

trip to Germany in 1912, Felkin and his family travelled to New
Zealand, where they founded the Smaragdum Thalasses Temple
at Hawkes Bay. In 1916, before leaving for New Zealand for good,
Felkin founded three Temples: Hermes No. 28 at Bristol (his
numbering seems to have become quite random); Merlin in
London, for ex-members of Isis-Urania who also happened to be
Anthroposophists; and The Secret College in London, which was
restricted to members of the S.R.I.A. To this last came Carnegie
Dickson, who had left Brodie-Innes and returned, as predicted,
to Felkin. He also acquired Miss C. M. Stoddart, who became
successively Imperatrix of the Amoun Temple and a sufferer
from paranoid delusions. She came to believe that the Golden
Dawn was a manifestation of occult forces bent on destroying
Christian civilization and accepted absolutely the reality of Felkin's astral entities, but with a vastly different view of their nature.
Her delusions, interspersed with a great deal of extremely valuable documentary material on the Stella Matutina, were published in 1930 under the title *Light-bearers of Darkness* and using
the pseudonym of 'Inquire Within'. A sequel, *The Trail of the
Serpent*, was published in 1936.

Prior to her rule the Amoun Temple had as its Imperator the
Revd A. H. E. Lee, who had been a member of Isis-Urania and
was still a close friend of A. E. Waite. By 1915 Waite had set up a
completely new Order, the Fellowship of the Rosy Cross, complete with an Inner Order that he called the Ordo Sanctissimus
Roseae et Aureae Crucis. Into this Order he brought numbers of
his Masonic friends and a selection of occult-minded ladies from
Theosophical circles; he kept very few of the old Isis-Urania
members even though he still looked on many of them as personal
friends.

A. H. E. Lee was at this time busy compiling, with the aid of
D. H. S. Nicholson, yet another of Waite's Order members, the
Oxford Book of English Mystical Verse. Their work as editors
brought them into contact with a young man at the Oxford
University Press named Charles Williams, whose evident interest
in ritual, in mysticism and in Waite's poems led Lee to send him
on to Waite. It has commonly been assumed that Charles Williams met Waite when he moved to London in 1917, but he first
visited Waite's home on 4 September 1915—two years before his
Reception as a Neophyte in the F∴R∴C∴ at the Equinox
Ceremony on 21 September 1917. Frater Qui Sitit Veniat, as he

became, remained in the Order for eleven years—Waite's last diary reference to him is in 1928—and possibly much longer, for other members still recalled him in 1966. He would have been one of a band of faithful Rosicrucians who followed the Order's Temple as it lurched from one damp Kensington flat to another, fetching up at last in a room above the Yarker Library in Maida Vale.

Even though it lacked a permanent home the F∴R∴C∴ did not lack for rituals, for Waite began to print them in 1916 and never got around to stopping; even on his deathbed, in 1942, he was preparing a revision of the rites of his Inner Order. The rituals themselves are so ponderous and unexciting that there was no risk whatever of another Temple purloining them, but the outlines of the Order workings *were* appropriated by Alvin Langdon Coburn, the photographer, who fell out with Waite in 1922 when he utilized the robes and some of the Temple settings of the F∴R∴C∴ for the Universal Order which he was then engaged in reorganizing. (Its purpose was—and is—the teaching of Platonic philosophy; it has no ritual workings.)

Few, if any, of Waite's members made an impact upon contemporary occultism but the Stella Matutina moulded two of the three most influential writers on magic of this century, Dion Fortune and Israel Regardie. (The third, Aleister Crowley, moulded himself and so much has already been written about him that it would be pointless to say any more.)

Dion Fortune, under her real name of Violet Firth—her pen-name was derived from her Order motto 'Dea Non Fortuna'—joined the London Temple of Brodie-Innes' Alpha and Omega in 1919, working under Maiya Curtis-Webb (later to be Mrs Tranchell-Hayes), whom she took as a model for her fictional heroine Vivian le Fay Morgan. For reasons never made clear (but assuredly not for the reasons implied in Crowley's scurrilous poem about Maiya:

> Mrs Webb does what she can,
>   As a lusty Lesbian,
> To make a Sappho of the filly,
>   Who never trots in Piccadilly;
> Girl to Girl and man to man,
>   Is part of her plan . . . [and so on, *ad nauseam*][6]

she did not stay long with Maiya and entered the other A.·.O
Temple set up by Mina Mathers who had returned to London
after her husband's death in 1918.

Here she remained for some years, founding the Fraternity of
the Inner Light in 1922 as a means of drawing new, younger
members into the Order via the Theosophical Society. Eventually
Mina Mathers expelled her:

> It may be as well to explain my own position in relation to the 'Golden
> Dawn'. I joined the Southern Branch of the Scottish section of it,
> since disbanded, in 1919 and transferred from there to the section of it
> of which Mrs McGregor Mathers was the head, and which claimed
> the only orthodoxy. She nearly turned me out for writing *The Esoteric
> Philosophy of Love and Marriage*, on the grounds that I was betraying
> the inner teaching of the Order, but it was pointed out to her that I had
> not then got the degree in which the teaching was given, and I was
> pardoned. She suspended me for some months for writing *Sane
> Occultism*, and finally turned me out because certain symbols had not
> appeared in my aura—a perfectly unanswerable charge. However, I
> transferred again to yet another section of the Order, where, for the
> first time, I saw justice done to what it is, in my opinion, a very great
> system, and continued my studies without interruption.[7]

This other section was the Stella Matutina, whose Hermes
Temple she joined, possibly because it had become, in 1923, an
independent Temple. (Miss Stoddart, however, claimed that she
and her fellow Chiefs had merely 'released them from our authority'; Felkin had given them their independence by cable.) In
time Dion Fortune set up a Temple of her own at Queens-
borough Terrace, the headquarters of the Inner Light, in which
her former Chief of Hermes (Hope Hughes) became convinced
that she worked Black Magic. Black or otherwise she continued
writing about magic and became one of the few magicians to earn
a successful living from her books.

In this she was equalled by her fellow Hermes initiate, Israel
Regardie. As a young man Regardie had acted for a time as
secretary to Aleister Crowley, whom he greatly admired; as a
result of Crowley's influence he produced his first two books, *A
Garden of Pomegranates* (1930) and *The Tree of Life* (1932). The latter
contained much material from the Golden Dawn, albeit filtered
through Crowley, and before its publication Regardie sent the
rough draft to Maiya Tranchell-Hayes, who had previously

loaned him some magical manuscripts. In a letter he told her: 'I have the utmost respect for your magical knowledge. The Adeptus Minor degree of the G.D. was awarded not for nothing, I know. Hence your criticisms will be worth much more to me.' Probably they were not, for the Chiefs of the A.·.O.·. were unhappy at seeing their system published, and in 1934 Regardie transferred his allegiance to the Stella Matutina.

Even here he became disillusioned by the opposition of elderly members to practical magic. Dismayed by an ossified system, Regardie determined to risk their deadly and hostile currents of will—deeming these to be equally ossified—and began, in 1936, to publish 'The Teachings, Rites and Ceremonies of the Order of the Golden Dawn'. By the time the fourth volume had appeared in 1940 many members of the Stella Matutina had become reconciled to the work—if only for the practical reason that the existence of a printed ritual removed the need for manual copying. A further result of his action was the birth of 'The Brothers of the Path', a movement founded in Yorkshire by Anthony Greville-Gascoigne; it was inspired by Regardie's works, devoted to the promotion of his type of occultism, and it published a journal called *The Golden Dawn*, to which Regardie contributed a justification of his work. But the journal, the Brotherhood and its ideals all vanished in the Second World War.

None of the original Temples survived—the Hermes Temple in Bristol lasted longest, dying in 1972 with its last chief, who protested to the end the non-existence of the rival Hermanubis Temple described by Francis King. My own efforts to find it went no further than an accommodation address in the Balls Pond Road and I believe it to have been no more than a chimaera. Other, more recent innovations exist, claiming descent from the cipher manuscripts, and the various offshoots of the old Order that straggled across the Atlantic still survive in the form of Paul Foster Case's Brotherhood of the Adytum. But Mathers has gone, Felkin has gone and Waite has gone. Perhaps only the Secret Chiefs remain.

In 1966 a box was found on the beach near Selsey Bill which had fallen from the cliffs in which it had been buried. It contained the robes, banners and magical instruments of Maiya Tranchell-Hayes, but High Magic was quite unknown to the experts to whom the finders took it. They said that 'the contents had probably belonged to a witch'. Such is the reward of the Hermetic Student.

References:
1. The Manifesto is printed as Appendix G of this book.
2. A. E. Waite, *Shadows of Life and Thought* (1938), p. 184.
3. [C. M. Stoddart], *Light Bearers of Darkness* (1930), p. 87.
4. ibid., p. 91.
5. See Howe, *Magicians of the Golden Dawn*, p. 267.
6. Quoted in Kenneth Grant *The Magical Revival*, p. 177.
7. Dion Fortune, 'Ceremonial Magic Unveiled', in *The Occult Review*, Vol. 57. No. 1 (January 1933), p. 22.

7. Kingdom

The Golden Dawn gave birth to magicians, charlatans and eccentrics of many kinds, but it did not produce a single man or woman of genius. Yeats was unquestionably profoundly influenced by the Order, but his poetic genius would have flowered whatever path he had taken, while Mathers brought his magical genius fully fledged to the Order. Others, however industrious, fascinating or influential, did not affect the mainstream of English literature, art or thought; but they did create many curious byways, exploring them with the aid of the principles and practices of the Golden Dawn, and these byways have kept their fascination for dreamers and critics alike.

In literature the most enduring of these byways is within the genre of occult fiction, for while ghost stories and fairy tales have always been with us, tales of sorcery and supernatural evil set in the real world of the present were something new to the reading public at the turn of the century. Truly 'occult' fiction may be said to have begun with *Dracula* (1897), and the enormous popularity of this tale of vampires and evil powers undoubtedly encouraged publishers to take up similar fiction from other, less known authors. *Dracula* itself cannot be laid at the door of the Golden Dawn, for Bram Stoker (despite popular claims to the contrary) was never a member, but he was a friend of Brodie-Innes and they did discuss their mutual interest in the dark side of occultism.

The true forte of the *literati* of the Golden Dawn was in producing tales that depended for their effect upon an unquestioning acceptance of the reality of supernatural forces and the validity of rituals designed to control them. These stories are invariably structured around a hero who fills the role of a supremely wise Initiate or, more frequently, a 'psychic detective', using his occult training to solve supernatural problems and to combat earthly and unearthly evil. Without the existence of the Golden Dawn such fiction could not have been written, so closely does it depend on the activities and ideas prevalent in the Order; and it deserves examining in depth, for its place in the history of popular fiction has never been critically assessed.

The first author to bring the Order to the aid of his fiction was Algernon Blackwood, whose hero, John Silence, was modelled on a real member of the Golden Dawn, but one it has not been possible to identify save by the initials that appear in the dedication of *John Silence, Physician Extraordinary* (1908): 'To M.L.W. the original of John Silence and my companion in many adventures'. Blackwood was a member of Waite's faction of the Golden Dawn after 1903 but he had joined in 1900 so that he would have been familiar with the rituals and the ethos of the Order when still in its magical state.

The hero of his tales is an ideal Rosicrucian, healing the spiritually sick without charge and evidently trained by more traditional Rosicrucians than those of the Golden Dawn:

> In order to grapple with cases of this peculiar kind, he had submitted himself to a long and severe training, at once physical mental and spiritual. What precisely this training had been, or where undergone, no one seemed to know,—for he never spoke of it, as, indeed, he betrayed no single other characteristic of the charlatan,—but the fact that it had involved a total disappearance from the world for five years, and that after he returned and began his singular practice no one ever dreamed of applying to him the so easily acquired epithet of quack, spoke much for the seriousness of his strange quest and also for the genuineness of his attainments.[1]

Faced by an attack from the wicked spirit of an evil woman, in *A Psychical Invasion*, John Silence utilizes concepts that his creator learned in the Golden Dawn:

> He began to breathe deeply and regularly, and at the same time to absorb into himself the forces opposed to him, and to *turn them to his*

own account. By ceasing to resist, and allowing the deadly stream to pour into him unopposed, he used the very power supplied by his adversary and thus enormously increased his own.

For this spiritual alchemy he had learned. He understood that force ultimately is everywhere one and the same; it is the motive behind that makes it good or evil; and his motive was entirely unselfish. He knew—provided that he was not first robbed of self-control—how vicariously to absorb these evil radiations into himself and change them magically into his own good purposes. And, since his motive was pure and his soul fearless, they could not work him harm'.[2]

In *Secret Worship* the victim is saved from soul-destruction by recalling the face of John Silence:

It was a face of power . . . of simple goodness . . . And, in his despair and abandonment, he called upon it, and called with no uncertain accents. He found his voice in this overwhelming moment to some purpose; though the words he actually used, and whether they were in German or English, he could never remember. Their effect, nevertheless, was instantaneous. The Brothers understood, and that grey Figure of evil understood.

For a second the confusion was terrific. There came a great shattering sound. It seemed that the very earth trembled. But all Harris remembered afterwards was that voices rose about him in the clamour of terrified alarm—

'A man of power is among us! A man of God!'

The vast sound was repeated—the rushing through space as of huge projectiles—and he sank to the floor of the room, unconscious.[3]

The idea of the powerful White Magician was to be frequently used by later writers, as was the essential explanation, in occult terms, of what had happened. In this case John Silence explains that the devil-worshippers were 'a concourse of the shells of violent men, spiritually-developed but evil men, seeking after death—the death of the body—to prolong their vile and unnatural existence. And had they accomplished their object, you, in turn, at the death of your body, would have passed into their power and helped to swell their dreadful purposes'[4]—an idea taken, of course, from *Dracula*, for this is the manner in which vampires gain recruits. Magicians are nothing if not eclectic.

Even more mystically inclined writers utilized magic when it suited their needs. Thus, in *The Column of Dust* (1909), Evelyn

Underhill, who was a member of Waite's Independent and
Rectified Rite, brought the spirit who becomes inescapably linked
to her heroine into its possession by the working of ritual magic.
Seeking knowledge, the heroine, ignorant of all occultism,
attempts to work a ritual from the *Grand Grimoire* in the bookshop
where she works. As the ritual progresses the author explains the
theory behind it: 'Hence the last clauses of the incantation came
from her lips with an imperious ring which was appropriate
enough to that superb procession of Divine names by which the
student of magic really compels himself to exaltation, whilst he
purports to be compelling the spirits of the air.'[5] A slip of paper
hidden in the Grimoire gives yet more of the received wisdom of
the Golden Dawn: 'Lo, my beloved son and very dear disciple, I
bequeath to thee this Grimoire, the companion of my labours,
wherein are faithfully set forth the true Rituals of Magic, together
with all things needful for the prosecution of that most divine
experiment on which thou art set: to wit, the Word, the Sign, and
the Way. Guard well that secret knowledge, remembering the
four oaths of thy initiation: to Dare, to Will, to Learn, and to
Conceal. But as to this book, have no fear lest the profane and
those unlearned in Philosophie discover aught therein, since,
even as the Ark within the Temple, all truth here dwells behind
a veil; which veil the priests of the Hidden Wisdom alone may
pass . . .'[6]

The heroine discovers, too, the value of sounds and calls:
'Constance was now impelled to chant, in a loud tone and with a
grave intense and crescent determination, the strange old Hebrew spell. The words drew from her—she knew not for what
reason—a long and rhythmic cry; a wailing music, with curious
ululative prolongations of the vowel sounds. It came from some
obscure corner of her spirit, which thus found for the first time a
language suited to its needs.'[7] And the ritual has worked, for the
spirit has been trapped inside her being even though she is
unaware of its presence: 'It was evidently true, as Eliphas Lévi had
said, and the best modern occultists agreed, that magical operations did have some curious effect upon the mind. She could not
recover her normal poise; things wore an unusual air, and she was
an alien amongst them. She decided that she would go to bed
early; she was not in the mood for sitting alone that night.

She had yet to realize that she would never be alone any more.'[8]

From such beginnings magical fiction slipped out of the hands of Golden Dawn magicians, to be treated well by some and dismally by others, reaching its nadir in the lurid nonsense foisted on to the public in the guise of the Black Magic tales of Dennis Wheatley, a blow from which neither the genre itself nor the critical acumen of the public has ever recovered. But there were other and better writers more directly influenced by those offshoots of the Golden Dawn to which they belonged.

Of these Dion Fortune, as Violet Firth preferred to be known, stuck most closely to magic proper. She further modelled her fictional characters upon real magicians, although she did allow credulity to get the better of her, and her novels and short stories all suffer from a surfeit of theosophic pseudo-wisdom. Neither the spectacular occult powers nor the exalted previous incarnations of Vivian le Fay Morgan, the heroine of *The Sea Priestess* and of *Moon Magic*, are likely to have been claimed or possessed by her original, Maiya Tranchell-Hayes. Mrs Hayes was a member of the Stella Matutina but was more closely aligned with the mystical than with the magical tradition; yet she appears to have been Dion Fortune's earliest occult mentor. It is probable, however, that her model for 'Dr Taverner' was a magician in the true sense, for in the Preface to *The Secrets of Dr. Taverner* (1926) she states: 'To "Dr Taverner" I owe the greatest debt of my life; without "Dr Taverner" there would have been no "Dion Fortune"'. This psychic detective was was a medical practitioner with a nursing home near Hindhead; in reality it was outside Guildford and the doctor's real name was Moriarty—an apt name, for his flouting of conventional morality places him on a par with the villainous adversary of Sherlock Holmes, whose namesake he was. He does not seem to have achieved outward prominence in the Stella Matutina, to which Dion Fortune belonged, but if there is truth in the claim that 'these stories, far from being written up for the purposes of fiction have been toned down to make them fit for print', then Dr Moriarty indeed dwelt on the plane of the Secret Chiefs.

The most entertaining story, and the only one to reveal anything, albeit obliquely, about the ritual workings of the Stella Matutina is *The Power House*. This tale concerns the activities of a spurious occultist who acts as a psychic leech upon the women who are lured into his sham magical order. Josephus, the occultist, is evidently—and unkindly—modelled upon Aleister Crowley, and Dion Fortune's dislike of Crowley's lifestyle is apparent in her description of him: 'Josephus is not a trained occultist, but he knows a great deal about the secret side of both sex and drugs, and he is a very clever manipulator of human nature and loves intrigue for its own sake, as this scheme of his shows.'[9] Dr Taverner defeats Josephus and disperses his followers by appearing in their Temple as a true Magus:

> Taverner opened his suitcase and took out the most wonderful robes I have ever seen in my life. Stiff with embroidery and heavy with bullion, the great cope looked like the mines of Ophir in the shaded light of that sombre room. Taverner put it on over an emerald green soutane and I fastened the jewelled clasp upon his breast. Then he handed to me, for he could not raise his arms, the Head-dress of Egypt, and I placed it on his head. I have never seen such a sight. The gaunt lineaments of Taverner framed in the Egyptian drapery, his tall figure made gigantic by the cope, and the jewelled ankh in his hand ... made a picture which I shall remember to my dying day.[10]

This is virtually a picture of Mathers and his manner is as autocratic as that of Mathers when he addresses the lodge: ' "The name of the Council of Seven has been invoked, and I who am the Senior of Seven, have come unto you. Know me by this sign," and he extended his hand. On the fore-finger flashed a great ring.'[11] He deconsecrates the Temple and Josephus is finished:

> Taverner returned to the altar ... then from under his cope he produced a curiously wrought metal box. He opened one end and took out of it a handful of white powder and strewed it upon the altar in the form of a cross.
> 'Unclean', he said, and his voice was like the tolling of a bell.
> He opened the other end of the box and took out a handful of ashes, and these also he strewed upon the altar, defiling its white linen covering.
> 'Unclean,' he said again. He stretched forth his ankh, and with the head of it extinguished the lamp that burnt upon the altar.
> 'Unclean,' he said a third time, and as he did so, all sense of power seemed to leave the room, and it became flat, ordinary and rather tawdry. Taverner alone seemed real, all the rest were make-believe.[12]

For those who knew the Golden Dawn and its magicians the message was clear—Mathers served the Good and True, Crowley the false and evil.

Crowley, of course, served as a model Magus for many writers—for Somerset Maugham in *The Magician*, for M. R. James in *Casting the Runes*, even for himself in *Moonchild* (1929), where his fellow magicians of the Golden Dawn, all thinly disguised, appear as incompetent but vicious necromancers battling against the holy magic of Cyril Grey/Simon Iff, who is Crowley. He probably named himself after Simon Magus, who, to Crowley's inverted way of thinking, represented all that is good in a magician.

To Charles Williams, however, Simon Magus was the antithesis of good, and the one true Black Magician in his novels is duly called Simon the Clerk. He it is who seeks world dominion in William's last novel, *All Hallows Eve* (1945), and he uses a central theme of the Golden Dawn system, the utterance of Words of Power:

His books and divinations had told him, and the lesser necromantic spells he had before now practised on the dead had half-shown him, what he might expect to see. As he approached after the graded repetitions, the greatest and most effective repetition—and the very centre of that complex single sound—he expected, visible before him, the double shape; the all but dead body, the all but free soul. They would be lying in the same space, yet clearly distinct, and with the final repetition of the reversed Name they would become still more distinct, but both at his disposal and subject to his will. He would divide without dis-uniting, one to go and one to stay, the spiritual link between them only just not broken, but therefore permanent.[13]

Necessarily he fails and is finally vanquished—as are all professors of wickedness in Williams' novels, whether they seek to defile the Holy Grail, to master the true Tarot, or to seize the Stone of Solomon. In each case the theme of the novel is drawn from concepts that Williams could, and probably did, find in A. E. Waite's Fellowship of the Rosy Cross, but the elegant structure of his work and the peculiar orthodoxy of his theology are Williams' own—the Golden Dawn was always his servant, never his master.

In like manner Arthur Machen was little influenced by the Order. His stories of spiritual horror were more concerned with the perversion of spiritual alchemy than with magic and were mostly written before he entered the Order. It is more probable that his awareness of a supernatural realm interpenetrating our world, often with malevolent intent, drew him into the Golden

Dawn rather than that his membership of the Order helped to develop these ideas within him. But he may have gained elements of his stories from discussions with A. E. Waite and other members of the Order, and the stimulus given to tales of magic by the continued existence of the Golden Dawn undoubtedly led to the continuing public demand for Machen's own tales.

The only certain case of the ideas and practices of the Golden Dawn moulding the whole work of an author is that of Algernon Blackwood. Elemental forces, ancient worship, Egyptian settings and the doctrines of Karma and Reincarnation that permeate his work may have been drawn from other sources, but they were the stock in trade of the Golden Dawn and he was an active member for at least ten years. One novel, *The Human Chord* (1910), is built solely around the desire for forbidden knowledge: the true uttering of the Tetragrammaton, the hidden name of God. The magician of the story is a clergyman, improbably called Philip Skale, who seeks the aid of two occult innocents to further his design of uttering the Word of Power. Unlike the characters of Evelyn Underhill or Charles Williams who are similarly concerned with magical utterance, he is neither ignorant nor evil. He explains his theory to his assistant:

'By repeating your outer name in a certain way until it disappears in the mind, I can arrive at the real name within. And to utter it is to call upon the secret soul—to summon it from its lair. . . . By certain rhythms and vibratory modulations of the voice it is possible to produce harmonics of sound which awaken the inner name into life—and then to spell it out. Note well, to *spell* it, spell—incantation—the magical use of sound—the meaning of the Word of Power used with such grand effect in the old forgotten Hebrew magic. Utter correctly the names of their Forces, or Angels . . . pronounce them with full vibratory power that awakens all the harmonics, and you awaken also their counterpart in yourself; you summon their strength or characteristic quality to your aid; you introduce their powers actively into your own psychical being.'[14]

Later, he describes the method to be used:

'When the Letters move of themselves and make the first sign, we shall know it beyond all doubt of question. At any moment of the day or night it may come. Each of you then hasten to your appointed place and wait for the sound of my bass in the cellar. There will be no mistake about it; you will hear it rising through the building. Then, each in turn, as it reaches you, lift your voices and call your notes. The chord thus rising through the building will gather in the flying Letters: it will unite them; it will summon them down to the fundamental master-tone I utter in the cellar. The moment the Letter summoned by each particular voice reaches the cellar, that voice must cease its utterance. Thus, one by one, the four mighty Letters will come to rest below. The gongs will vibrate in sympathetic resonance; the colours will tremble and respond; the finely drawn wires will link the two, and the lens of gas will lead them to the wax, and the record of the august and terrible syllable will be completely chained. At any desired moment afterwards I shall be able to reawaken it . . .

'But . . . remember that once you have uttered your note, you will have sucked out from the Letter a portion of its own resistless force, which will immediately pass into yourself. You will instantly absorb this, for you will have called upon a mighty name—the mightiest—and your prayer will have been answered . . . *We shall be as Gods!*'[15]

And this is the very essence of the system and its rituals: to be more than human and to be equal with God.

Philip Skale inevitably fails in his attempt and is destroyed, but he had come perilously close to success, and it was this ability to achieve, or almost to achieve, what was impossible for ordinary mortals that encouraged the very ordinary mortals who were the magicians of the Golden Dawn to turn these dreams into fiction and to act out in fantasy what could not be acted out in fact.

Outside the realm of fiction, of overt fiction at least, members of the Order produced books in abundance—some wise, some foolish, mostly verbose. The prodigious output of both Waite and Crowley owed much to the Golden Dawn, as did the smaller, but no less important, floods of words from Mathers, Westcott and a dozen others. Much of their work is now of no value, as, indeed, was the case when they were first published, but many remarkable books have survived and their importance has been recognized. Even while scholars decry the academic value of Mathers' *The Kabbalah Unveiled* (1887) they cannot deny its seminal influence upon the study of Jewish mysticism, as they cannot deny the equal importance of Waite's study, *The Holy Kabbalah* (1929). But the literary influence of the Golden Dawn, beyond this narrow field of scholarship, was small and less by far than has often been claimed.

And could a magical Order have any significance for the world of philosophy or for the world of art? It could not and it did not. Both artists and philosophers appeared among the members, but they came to the Order fully clothed with their disciplines and fully clothed they left it. W. T. Horton and Pamela Colman Smith certainly drew upon magical ideas for the content of their work—as did Austin Osman Spare, but he only touched the Order at second hand—but their respective styles were born of the Art Nouveau movement and owed nothing to the idiosyncratic notions of ancient Egyptian art dreamed up by Mathers for decorating the temples and vaults of the Order. The Tarot cards used by the Order, and those designed later for Waite by Pamela Colman Smith, may have influenced more recent occultists in search of inspired interpretations of Tarot symbolism, but their artistic influence has—fortunately—been non-existent.

C. D. Broad is alleged to have been a member of the Hermes Temple in Bristol, but none of his philosophical work, or his studies in psychical research, betray the slightest sign of the metaphysics of the Golden Dawn. Similarly, Evelyn Underhill's philosophy of mysticism runs entirely contrary to the ideas of the Order, for it was developed after she had cast off the Order and all its theories—with which she had never had any sympathy, even in the sanitized form presented to members of Waite's rectified Isis-Urania Temple. Had the thinking of the Order affected anyone it would have been Jung, but he seems not so much as to have ignored it as to have been utterly unaware of its existence.

Only in the field of occultism proper has the Golden Dawn shown its power, and that largely because of the stagnation of thought in the Theosophical Society. With the spread of popular journalism, occultism came into its own; in 1905 *The Occult Review* appeared, to present a non-sectarian range of esoteric knowledge and to provide, all unknown to its editor, a platform for the Golden Dawn. From that time on the stream of ideas, in books and articles, on every aspect of magical thought has never ceased, although scholarship and common-sense have diminished in proportion to the distance in years from the time that the Order flourished. Israel Regardie has given the workings of the Order, and the theories behind them, to the occult world at large, and imitators have followed behind him. Foolishness and palpable falsehood are offered to a public who read and believe them. Modern occult fraternities, of doubtful parentage, loudly proclaim the immense antiquity of beliefs that originated with Westcott and Mathers, their follies multiply and fictions about the Order's history are taken up eagerly by conspiracy theorists who see the little people of the Golden Dawn as gigantic villains in a monstrous Satanic plot to overthrow Christian civilization.

This is the unfortunate legacy of the Golden Dawn. From innocent speculation on Hermetic philosophy and harmless dabbling in quasi-magical ritual, a myth has grown up of ultimate Truths hidden from the multitude but readily available to the initiate. The everyday people who *were* the Golden Dawn are seen now through a distorting lens, and their essential humanity is taken from them. For those who wish to find it, the Hermetic philosophy that the Order propagated does have a value; but it is not to be found by adoring the framework of the Golden Dawn. Rather should one seek to understand the motivations of the members and to examine the kernel of rational thought that lay, and still lies, within their system. There was sense as well as nonsense in the Golden Dawn, and only by preserving and building upon that sense will the Hermetic Order of the Golden Dawn be seen as something more than a monument to human folly.

Vale, fratres et sorores!

References:
1. Algernon, Blackwood, *John Silence, Physician Extraordinary* (1908), pp. 3–4.
2. ibid., p. 64.
3. ibid., p. 282.
4. ibid., p. 289.
5. Evelyn Underhill, *The Column of Dust* (1909), p. 12.
6. ibid., p. 15.
7. ibid., p. 16.
8. ibid., p. 19.
9. Dion Fortune, *The Secrets of Dr. Taverner*, 3rd edition (1979), p. 223.
10. ibid., p. 226.
11. ibid., p. 227.
12. ibid., p. 228.
13. Charles Williams, *All Hallows Eve* (1945), p. 145.
14. Algernon Blackwood, *The Human Chord* (1910), p. 104.
15. ibid., p. 277.

Appendices

Appendix H Constitution of the R.R. et A.C., November 1903.

Appendix A

The Anna Sprengel Letters

1. *Recd. Nov. 26/87*

Dear Brother Sapere Aude,
I have long since left the place where you sent my letter but I did get your letter in the end after a long time. I was very pleased to hear that the secret papers described by you have once more come to light. These papers were lost years ago by the esteemed Abbé Constant and then came into the possession of two Englishmen who applied for permission to use them.

This was granted to the Society No. 2 of Hermanubis but we never heard whether anything useful was done there.

After you have managed to make a thorough examination of the papers and have understood them, it is within my competence to promote you and I appoint you to the $7° = 4°$ of the Second Order of the G.D. in England, L'Aube Dorée in France, Die Goldene Dämmerung in Germany.

You will now start a new society (No.) 3 and choose two learned persons in order to make up the first three Masters and when you have appointed three more as $5° = 6°$ Adepts you can then be independent.

Hermetic science is almost extinct in our own day and age, we ourselves are very few here but we are very zealous and earnest and possess considerable strength.

However, we are very cautious and do not entrust any letters to the post so can send you few communications and can be of little assistance.

Please write to me again and kindly seal the letter you send addressed to me, enclosing it in an envelope which is addressed to the Lodge of Light, Love and Life (Licht Liebe Leben), the address of which you know.

I remain in love,
Sap. Dom. Ast. $7 = 4$
My secretary 'In Utroque Fidelis' usually writes on my behalf.

2. ♀ *Jan 25/88*

To Brother 'Non Omnis Moriar'.
I give thee the authority to sign my device

Sapiens Dom. Ast.

on any paper if the need arise, in order to comply with my wishes and to form associations and to make ready the work of the Order G.D.

Yours faithfully,
Sap. Dom. Ast. ⑦ = 4°

3. *7 February 1888*

Dear Brother,
I am much pleased with your report to me and of your success in finding good members; let all reports and questions come from yourself only.

I send you as a curiosity pages written by A.N.V.T. [i.e. Eliphas Lévi]. Another eminent old Frather called 'Igne' has just died at Naples.

Yours with fraternal love,
Sap. Dom. Ast. $7 = 4$.

4. *Recd. Sept. 17/88*   *12 September 1888*

Esteemed Brother 'Sapere Aude' ⑤ = ⑥
Since it is impossible for me to attend your Ceremonies of the Equinox, I shall be with you in spirit.

I am delighted to hear that you are working all four Degrees of the first Order. You will need some of my papers in order to complete the Adept Degrees which I shall send you with all haste.

Greet my and your members and accept my hearty greeting.

Sap. Dom. Ast.   Chief Adept.

5. *Oct. 9 ♀ 1889*

Sapere Aude 5 = 6

Care Frater,

I was very pleased to hear that your training of new members has been successful and that four of these have reached the necessary degree of knowledge to enter the Second Order and to learn that your three Chiefs have named them Adepts 5 = 6.

As agreed, I declare your three Chiefs to have independent authority.

I am sending you with this letter a few old secret manuscripts and a few very ancient illustrations used in the various Orders.

I send you my best wishes for the happy success of the Golden Dawn Order.

I remain as ever your true, in the Order of (Chesed).

Sap. Dom. Ast. 7 = 4

6. *In nomine C.R.* [i.e. Christian Rosenkreuz]
Mon [te] *Ab* [iegno] *Dec* [embris] *XII Die 4 1889*

The Degree of 7 = 4 Ad [eptus] Ex [emptus] in the Second Order is hereby conferred in full entitlement to the following Brothers:

1) Non Omnis Moriar
   (Sapere Aude 5 = 6)
   who is my sole correspondent among you
2) To Deo Duce Comite Ferro
   (S' R.M.D. 5 = 6)
3) To Vincit Omnia Veritas
   (Magna est Veritas 5 = 6)

You are entitled to have full supervision over the degrees 0.1.2.3.4.5. & 6 = 5

S.D.A.   7 = 4

Ordinis Ros. Rub. et Aur. Crucis and Gold. Dämm. 5 = 6

7. Dear Brother N.O.M.
I am very sorry to have to inform you of the death of our learned
friend S.D.A. $7 = 4$ whose loss is very hard for me. The death
occurred on 20 July in a place near to B. We are afraid that the
young man I.U.F., the secretary who has often written letters to
you for S.D.A. in recent years, will have to abandon his studies
and apply himself to business.

But all our wishes are with you, you can be sure.

I must inform you that the permission to conduct ceremonies in
big Lodges as you now do and as you had permission from S.D.A.
to do (was) against the wishes of several other Chiefs, who will not
correspond with you or give you help at present until they see what
sort of effect the change will have on the interests of this society.
Yet a few papers 5 and 6 the property of the late S.D.A. will be sent
to you. I am enclosing my private card but only for your own use.

I remain your true brother.

Ex uno disces omnes

$7 = 4$. O.R.R. et A.C.

Dahme August 23, 1890.

Appendix B

Historical Lecture

by

V. H. Frater Sapere Aude
Praemonstrator of Isis-Urania Temple

Some years have passed away since it was decided to revive the
Order of the G.D. in the Outer, an Hermetic Society whose
members are taught the principles of Occult Science, and the
practice of the Magic of Hermes; the decease during the second
half of the century of several eminent adepts and chiefs of the
Order, having caused a temporary dormant condition. Prominent
among these Adepts were Eliphaz Lévi, the greatest of modern
French Magi, Ragon, the author of several classical books on
occult subjects; Kenneth Mackenzie, author of the Masonic
Encyclopaedia, and Frederick Hockley, famous for his crystal
seeing and his MSS. These and other contemporary adepts
received their knowledge and power from predecessors of equal
and of greater eminence but of even more concealed existence.
Many of them received indeed the doctrines and system of
Theosophy, Hermetic Science and the Higher Alchemy from a
long series of practical workers whose origin is traced to the
Fratres R.C. of Germany, which association was founded by
Christian Rosenkreuz and his brethren so far back as 1398.
  Valentin Andrea, the German theologian and mystic, has left
us in his works, published in and after the year 1614, an account of

the doctrines and exoteric management of the R.C. Society. But even the revival of mysticism was but a new development of the vastly older wisdom of the Kabbalistic Rabbis and of the most ancient of all secret knowledge, the Magic of the Egyptians, in which the Bible itself tells us that Moses the founder of the Jewish System was 'learned', that is, in which he had been initiated.

Through the Hebrew Kabbalah we have indeed become possessed of more of the ancient wisdom than from any other source, for it must be borne in mind that the Hebrews were taught at one time by the Egyptians, and at a later date by the Chaldean Sages of Babylon. It is a very curious fact that the Classical nations, the Greek and the Roman, have handed down to us but slight glimpses of the Ancient Magic, and this is the more notable because Greece succeeded to the Mastership of Egypt and Rome to the Empire both of the Greeks and of the Jews. Greece indeed succeeded to a share of the Mysteries of the Egyptians, for the Eleusinian Mysteries were copies of those more ancient and solemn ceremonies of Isis, Osiris and Serapis, but they lacked the true Magic of Egypt, and further the classics retain but faint glimpses of even the Eleusinian Secrets. And these glimpses serve only to disclose the fact that the Eleusinian pupils were partly ignorant of the Isiac Mysteries, a notable example of which is seen in the use of the words Konx om Pax, of which even they knew not the meaning, the words being merely the Greek imitation of real ancient Egyptian words whose meaning has been a secret for centuries. Hence the nought equals nought grade of Neophyte is found to possess Egyptian characteristics and symbolism, and further an attentive study of the Higher Grades will reveal the source of much of the culture and illustrate the language of the late Eliphaz Lévi, through whose adeptship and advocacy the study of occultism has been popularized.

The first Order is a group of four Grades to each of which in succession Neophytes are admissable. When duly approved of by the Greatly Honoured Chiefs, after showing themselves possessed of sufficient aptitude and knowledge. Beyond them above are three Grades of Adepts forming the Second Order; these have the power of initiating students into the lower grades and of issuing Warrants for Temples such as that of Isis Urania. But highest of all in this most ancient scheme are the Great Rulers of the whole system, who severally sustain and govern the third

order, which includes three magic titles of Honour and Supremacy. These represent the Supernal Triad of the Sephiroth and are
shrouded and unapproachable to the profane, and to all others
but to the Chiefs of the Adepti; in case of a vacancy in this Order,
the Chief most learned and most famous Adept obtains by decree
the coveted Supremacy.

The scheme of the G.D. then is formed upon the type of the
Decad of the Sephiroth, the ten emanations of Deity, as figured in
the very ancient Kabbalah of the Hebrews, whose professors were
illuminated by the Higher Magic of the Ancient World. The
Grades of the first order will be found to be of Hebrew design and
inasmuch as the efflux of the time brought on the revelation of the
Christos, the Tiphereth, the Beauty of the Microprosopus, so
Christian design is reflected in the Higher degrees. The
Neophyte grade, and the 1st, 2nd, 3rd, and 4th grades, which this
present Isis Urania Temple is authorized to confer, after due
examination and approval in each case, possess Rituals and
secrets which had been received from the Greatly Honoured
Chief Adepts, and were placed by them in the care of V. H. Frater
'S.Rioghail Mo Dhream' an eminent Kabbalist, Hermetic Student and Magister of the Soc. Ros. in Anglia, for revision, and to
render them suitable for English students of the present day. The
wording and the working arrangements have alone been revised;
the foundation of the Sephirotic scheme and the relative dependence of its several parts, the secret names and references are
untouched and unaltered from the Cipher MSS which were
handed to V. H. Sapere Aude $5° = 6°$ (whose motto was at that
time Quod Scis Nescis) already an Adept and an Honorary
Magus of the Soc Ros in Anglia, some years before by a most
eminent and illuminated Hermetist (since dead) whose title was
Frater 'Vive Momor Lethi'. He had been for many years in
communication with prominent British and Foreign Adepts, and
he had enjoyed ample access to the writing of Eliphaz Lévi. This
collection of the MSS has since been supplemented by a varied
collection of MSS chiefly in cypher, which have been either given
or lent to the Chiefs of the temple by our Continental Fratres and
Sorores.

These MSS provided the Adepts who possessed the secret of
their occult meaning, with the ability to extend the order of the
G.D. in the Outer subject to the approval of the Chiefs of the
Second Order.

This approval having been obtained from the G.H. Soror 'Sap: Dom. Ast' in Germany, the Fratres 'Quod Scis Nescis', 'S.Rioghail Mo Dhream' and 'Magna est Veritas' the Supreme Magus of the Soc Ros in Anglia, were duly instructed to extend the Order in England, and this Temple was consecrated as a successor to Hermanubis No. 2 which had ceased to exist, owing to the decease of all its Chiefs. The Temple No. 1 of Licht, Liebe, Leben is a group of Continental Mystics who have not been in the habit of performing ceremonies in open lodge, but have conferred the Grades chiefly in private and in the presence of only two or three members. For this reason there is no accurate record of the names and rank of all their members and very great reticence is shewn by them in their communications.

Very soon after the formation of this Temple No. 3 permission was granted for the consecration of Osiris Temple No. 4 at Weston Super Mare under the rule of our Very Honoured Frater 'Crux dat Salutem' and the West of England has been assigned to him as a province. Almost at the same time the Horus Temple No. 5 under the rule of the V.H. Frater 'Vota Vita Mea' was also consecrated at Bradford in Yorkshire. These three Temples have now members not only in this country but in the United States, Hindustan, Palestine, Denmark etc.

It will be convenient if I now give you the name of our order in the several languages—In Hebrew the title is Chabrath Zerek Aour bokhr, which means Society of the Shining Light of the Dawn. While yet Latin was in universal use among persons of culture the name was Aurora. In Greek Eos Chryse. In French 'L'Aube Dorée'. In German the title is 'Die Goldene Dämmerung'.

Reference may now be made to the Rosicrucian Society which was reconstructed by Frater Robert Wentworth Little, a student of the Mysteries, assisted by Fratres Dr W. R. Woodman, Captain F. G. Irwin and Dr Kenneth Mackenzie. This Society which has branches in England, Scotland and the U.S. perpetuates the form of Rosicrucian initiation, which was conferred a hundred years ago in England and which is mentioned by Godfrey Higgins, in his famous work 'The Anacalypsis, or an attempt to withdraw the veil of the Saitic Isis'.

Frater Little was a student of the works of Lévi and was also an eminent Freemason and the Rosicrucian Society as revised by him, was made by intention and permission essentially Masonic, thus severing all connection with the many eminent adepts who have not been craftsmen.

History narrates to us the splendid mental achievements of Basil Valentine, Artephius, Nicholas Flamel, Pastellus, Petrus of Abano, Cardan, Gaffarelli, Jacob Behmen and Robert Fludd. The Society in the same manner fails to recognize any worth for occult research in women. This also is an innovation upon the scheme of the Ancient Mysteries in many of which, notably those of Isis, priestesses and virgin prophets were prominent ministers.

I wish indeed to call special attention to the fact that in several instances of the Ancient MSS written in Cipher, where reference is made to the Fratres and Sorores, the words 'her' or 'him' occur, thus clearly showing that in older times as at the present day, women rose to high rank and attainments in the Secret knowledge of the Order.

History is by no means silent in respect of the success of women in occult researches; mention may be made of Pernelle, the wife and fellow-worker of Nicholas Flamel, of Martin Bertheran, companion to the Baron Jean de Chatelet, who died about 1645, and of the widow lady (afterwards symbolized by him as Sophia—Heavenly Wisdom), fellow student and inspirer of Johann Georg Gichtel who died in 1700, famous as a Mystic Theosophist. The occultists of today do not need to be reminded of the Great Hermetists and Theosophists of our day, of Dr Anna Kingsford, of whom death prematurely robbed us. She was indeed illuminated by the Sun of Light, and no one who ever heard her lecture and discuss the Hermetic Doctrines will ever forget her learning or her eloquence, her beauty or her grace. Of Madame Blavatsky, the leader of the Theosophical Society, a modern prophet of Eosteric Buddhism—no occult student, however wide apart may be his or her own favoured path to wisdom, can fail to recognize in her, a master-mind in a woman's frame.

The Soc Ros in Anglia is, to some extent exoteric in its lower grades but its concerns are regulated by adepts of eminence (an inner circle) who still hold the Secret Knowledge of R.C. and in addition the special, concealed secret information in the English Society, in which, of course the Members of the G.D. have no claim nor part, although they move along parallel lines.

The Soc Ros and its branches in the several countries, and the G.D. Order both descended from the same parents and predecessors; the one developed into a masculine and masonic system;

the other retaining the ancient and more extended basis of the admission of all bona-fide students; rich or poor and without regard to sex, may alike go on and prosper without interfering with the tranquility of the other and can lead true and patient students who can Will—Dare—Learn and Be Silent to the
Summum Bonum
True Wisdom
and
Perfect Happiness.

Appendix C

Order of the M.·.R.·. in the Outer Grades

Ceremony of Reception in the O = O Grade of Neophyte

The Opening of the Temple:

The Members assemble, wearing the Insignia of the Order.
Hierophant (knocks):
All rise. The Kerux passes by N. to right front of Hierophant and raises his Wand, as he does at all announcements, facing W.
Hierophant: Fratres and *Sorores* of the Isis-Urania Temple of the M.·.R.·. *vel G.·.D.·.* assist me to open the Temple in the Grade of Neophyte.'
Kerux: 'Hekas! Hekas! Este bebeloi!'
   The Kerux returns to his place by the S. and W., giving the Grade Sign as he passes the Throne of the E. n.b. In all movements of officers and members the course of the Sun must be followed, as far as passing round the Altar is concerned, excepting in Reverse Procession. The salute of the Grade must also be given when passing immediately in front of the Hierophant and, within the Portal, on entering or leaving the Temple.

Hierophant: 'Frater Kerux, see that the Temple is properly guarded.'

   The Kerux gives one knock on the inner side of the door, without opening it, and the Sentinel replies in like manner with the hilt of his sword on the outer side.

Kerux: 'Very Honoured Hierophant, the Temple is properly guarded.'

Hierophant: 'Honoured Hiereus, guard the hither side of the portal and assure yourself that all present have witnessed the M.·.R.·. *vel* G.·.D.·..'

Hiereus (passing to door and standing with sword in front of it): 'Fratres and Sorores of the M.·.R.·., give the Signs of a Neophyte' (done). 'Very Honoured Hierophant, all present have witnessed the M.·.R.·.' (gives signs)

The Hiereus returns to his place.

Hierophant (repeating Signs): 'Let the number of officers in this grade and the nature of their offices be proclaimed once again, that the powers whereof they are images may be reawakened in the spheres of those present and in the sphere of this Order. Honoured Hiereus, how many are the principal officers of the Neophyte Grade?'

Hiereus: 'They are three: The Hierophant, the Hierus and the Hegemon.'

Hierophant: 'What have their names in common?'

Hiereus: 'The letter H, emblem of Breath and Life.'

Hierophant: 'How many are the Lesser Officers?'

Hiereus: 'They are 3 also: The Stolistes, the Dadouchos and the Kerux, with the Sentinel who stands armed outside, whose duties are to repel intruders and to prepare the Candidate.'

Dadouchos: 'My place is in the South with the Censer, as an image of heat and dryness. My duty is to see that the lamps and fires of the Temple are ready at the opening; to watch over the thurible and the incense; and to consecrate the Hall, the *Fratres* and *Sorores* and the Candidate by Fire.'

Stolistes: 'My station is in the North, with water and aspergillus, to signify cold and moisture. My duty is to see that the robes, collars and insignia of the officers are ready before the Opening; to watch over the cup of cleansing water; and to purify the Hall, the *Fratres* and *Sorores* and the Candidate with Water.'

Kerux: 'My place is on the hither side of the Portal. My duty is to see that the furniture of the Hall is properly arranged at the Opening; to guard the door from within; to admit *Fratres* and *Sorores*; to watch over the reception of Candidates; to lead all circumambulations, carrying the lamp of my office; and to make all announcements and reports. My lamp is the Image of the Light of Hidden Knowledge; my wand of its mastery over the heart and elements.'

Hegemon: 'My place is between the Pillars, and I preside over the symbolic gateway of the secret Knowledge. I am the Reconciliation between Light and Darkness. My white robe signifies purity. I bear a mitre-headed sceptre, emblematic of Religion which guides and regulates life and directs the higher aspirations of the Soul. My face is turned to the Cubical Altar of created things. I watch over the preparation of the Candidate; I assist in his reception; and I lead him in the Middle Path of the Candidate; I assist in his reception; and I lead him in the Middle Path which lies between the Darkness and the Light.'

Hiereus: 'My place is on the Throne of the West, as an Image of Darkness. My robe is black, to symbolize that darkness which dwelt upon the face of the Waters. I carry the Sword of Judgment and the Banner of the Evening Twilight. I am Darkness and the Master of Darkness, and I am called Fortitude by the unhappy. I keep the Gateway of the West; I watch over the work of the lesser officers and over the reception of the Candidate.'

Hierophant: 'My place is on the Throne of the East, symbolizing the Rising Sun. I rule and govern the Hall and its members of every grade, according to the Laws of the Order, as He whose Image I am governs all who work for the Hidden Knowledge. My robe is red because of uncreated Fire. I bear the sceptre and the Banner of the East. I am the Expounder of Mysteries. I am Power, Light, Mercy and Wisdom. *Frater Stolistes*, I direct you to purify the Hall and the Members with Water.'

The Stolistes passes to E., faces Hierophont, makes a cross with Cup and sprinkles thrice. He proceeds in succession to S.W. and N., facing each point, when he repeats cross and sprinkling. He completes circle by returning to E., where he faces Hierophant, uplifts cup and says:

Stolistes: 'I purify with Water.'

He salutes the Throne and returns to his place by S. and W.

Hierophant: '*Frater Dadouchos*, I direct you to consecrate the Hall and Members by Fire.'

The Dadouchos passes by W. and N. to E., faces Hierophant, salutes, raises Thurible, makes cross therewith and censes three times. He proceeds S., W. and N. facing each point, making cross as before and censing three times. He returns to E., uplifts Thurible and says:

Dadouchos: 'I consecrate with Fire.'

He again salutes the Throne and returns to his place direct.

Hierophant: 'Let the Mystical Procession take place in the Path of Light.'

The Kerux passes to N. and halts. The Hegemon passes by S. and W. where he is joined by Hiereus and they proceed, with Hegemon in front, to their places behind the Kerux. The Dadouchos follows Hegemon from S. to W. where he allows the Hiereus to step between and so passes to N. where he takes his place on the right of Stolistes. The Kerux, Hegemon, Hiereus, Stolistes and Dadouchos circumambulate the Temple with the sun. The Hiereus passes Hierophant once, the Hegemon twice and the rest three times when, after salutes, they return to their places with the sun.

Hierophant: 'The Mystical Procession is accomplished. Let us adore the Lord of the Universe.'

All present face E. and salute. The salute is maintained throughout the Adoration.

Hierophant: 'Holy art Thou, Lord of the Universe. Holy art Thou whom Nature hath not formed. Holy art Thou the Vast One and the Mighty, Lord of Light and Darkness.' (Then facing the W.) 'In His Name, Frater Kerux I command you to announce that the Temple is open.'

The Kerux, passing by N. to North front of the Throne of the Hierophant, raises his Wand, saying:

Kerux: 'In His Name who works in silence and only silence can express, I proclaim that the Sun has risen.'

Kierophant: 'Khabs' (knocks)
Hiereus: 'Am' (knocks)
Hegemon: 'Pekht' (knocks)
Hiereus: 'Konx' (knocks)
Hegemon: 'Om' (knocks)
Hierophant: 'Pax' (knocks)
Begemon: 'Light' (knocks)
Hierophant: 'in,' (knocks)
Hiereus: 'Extension' (knocks)

End of the Ceremony of the Opening of the Temple.

Ceremony of the Admission of a Neophyte

The Kerux removes the Rose, Lamp, Chalice and Paten from Altar.

Hierophant: '*Fratres* and *Sorores* of the Order of the $M \cdot R \cdot$. I have received a Dispensation from the Second Order to admit *A.B.* to the O = O Degree of Neophyte, in witness whereof I command the Honoured Hegemon to see that the Candidate is prepared.'

The Hegemon rises, removes his chair between the Pillars and passes without the Portal. He instructs the Sentinel to prepare the Candidate by hoodwinking him and passing a rope three times about his waist. He then proceeds to the door of the Temple and gives an alarm knock.

Kerux: (within) Knocks. 'The Candidate seeks admission.

Turns down lights.

Hierophant 'I give you permission to admit A.B. who will now lose his earthly name and will be known hereafter amongst us as *Frater Adveniat Regnum (vel alius)* Let the Stolistes and Dadouchos assist the Kerux in the Reception.'

The Door is opened by the Kerux who bars the entrance of the candidate when he is within the Portal.

Hegemon: 'Inheritor of the dying world, arise and enter the darkness!'
Stolistes: 'The Mother of the Darkness has blinded him with her hair.'
Dadouchos: 'The Father of the darkness has hidden him under his wings.'
Hierophant: 'His limbs are still weary from the war that was in heaven.'
Kerux: 'Child of Earth, unpurified and unconsecrated, you cannot enter the sacred Hall of the Neophytes.'

The Stolistes cross-marks the Candidate on the forehead and sprinkles him three times.

Stolistes: 'I purify you with Water.'

The Dadouchos makes a cross with thurible and censes three times.

Dadouchos: 'I consecrate you with Fire.'

If there is more than one Candidate the consecration of each with Fire and Water must be completed before proceeding to the next. The Stolistes and Dadouchos resume their places but remain standing.

Hierophant: 'Inheritor of the dying world, what do you seek among us?'
Hegemon (replying for Candidate): 'My soul wanders in the darkness, seeking for the Light of the Hidden Knowledge, and I believe that I shall find this Sacred Light among you.'
Hierophant: 'Place the Candidate at the West of the Altar.'

This is done by the Hegemon.

Hierophant: 'We hold your signed pledge to keep secret all things respecting this Order. To confirm it, I now ask whether you are willing to take a solemn obligation in the presence of our Assembly that you will keep inviolate the secrets and mysteries of this Order. There is nothing incompatible with your civil, moral or religious duties in this obligation, for although transcendental virtues may awake to a momentary life in foolish and wicked hearts, they cannot subsist in any unless the natural virtues are their throne. He who is the Foundation of Spirits comes not to break but to fulfil the Law. Are you ready to take this pledge?'

Candidate: 'I am ready.'

The Hierophant proceeds to the E. of the Altar, the Hiereus to the N.W., and the Hegemon to the S.W., the Three Officers thus forming a triangle. The Candidate is close to the Altar on the W. Members of all Grades rise and remain standing while the Obligation is taken.

Hierophant (to Candidate): 'You will kneel on both knees' (the Candidate is assisted accordingly). 'Give me your right hand which I place on this Holy Symbol; put your left hand in mine; bow your head; repeat your full name and say after me: *Hierophant* (followed by Candidate): 'I, A.B., in the presence of the Lord of Heaven and Earth and in the presence of this Hall of the Neophytes of the Order of the *M.·. R.·.*, regularly assembled under Warrant from the Second Order, do, of my own free will, most solemnly promise to keep this Order secret, its name, the names of its members and the proceedings which take place at its meetings from every person in the world who has not been initiated therein; nor will I discuss them with any member who has resigned, demitted, or been expelled. I promise solemnly to keep secret any information concerning it which I may have gathered before taking this oath. I promise solemnly, in like manner, to persevere with courage and determination in the labours of the Divine Science even as I shall persevere undaunted through this Ceremony which is their Image. I will not debase my mystical knowledge in the works of Evil Magic at any time or under any temptation. I undertake that all rituals or lectures placed in my care, with any cover containing them, shall bear the official lable of the *M.·. R.·.* I will neither copy nor allow to be copied any manuscripts of the *M.·. R.·.* until I have obtained a written permission from the Second Order, lest our Secret Knowledge become revealed through my neglect. I will not suffer myself to be placed in such a state of passivity that any uninitiated person or power may cause me to lose control of my words, thoughts or actions. I swear upon this Holy Symbol to observe all these points without evasion, equivocation or mental reservation, under the penalty of being expelled from the Order for my offence and perjury, and furthermore of submitting myself by this my own act, to a hostile current of will set in motion by the Divine Guardians of the Order, living in the light of their perfect justice, who can, as tradition and experience affirm, strike the breaker of the mystical obligation with death or palsy, or overwhelm him with misfortunes. They journey as upon the winds; they strike where no man strikes; they slay where no sword slays' [the Hiereus places his sword on the neck of the Candidate] 'and even as I bow my neck under the sword of the Hiereus, so do I commit myself into their hands for vengeance or reward.' [the sword is removed by the Hiereus] 'So help me my mighty and secret Soul, and the Father of my Soul, who works in silence and nought but silence can express.'

A pause.

Hierophant: 'Rise, Neophyte of the O = O Grade of the Order of the $M.\cdot.R.\cdot.$'.

(The German name is here given in full.) The Candidate is assisted accordingly, the Hierophant and Hiereus return to their places. All members are seated.

Hierophant: 'Honoured Hegemon, You will now place the Candidate in the Northern part of the Hall, the place of darkness, forgetfulness and necessity.'

This is done and the Candidate is faced to the East.

Hierophant: 'The voice of my Secret Soul spoke and said: Let me enter the Darkness that peradventure I may find the Light. I am the only being in an Abyss of Darkness. Therefrom came I forth ere my birth from the silence of a primal sleep. The Voice of Ages answered my Soul and said: 'I am He who formulates in Darkness. The light shineth in darkness, but the darkness comprehendeth it not.'

A pause.

Hierophant: 'Let the Candidate commence his passage from darkness into light, with the Lamp of the Hidden Knowledge to guide him.'

The Dadouchos passes by W. to N. and when he has passed on the right of the Stolistes, the Kerux takes his place in front of Hegemon and Candidate. The Kerux and Hegemon leading the Neophyte, with the Stolistes and Dadouchos pass round by E. with Sol, for the first time, no alarm being given by the Hierophant. The Hiereus knocks once as the procession passes the West (Knocks) The Hierophant knocks once as it passes the E. for the second time (Knocks) The Kerux then halts in the S. and, turning round, bars the way, saying:

Kerux: 'Child of Earth, unpurified and unconsecrated, you cannot enter the Path of the West.'

The Stolistes cross-marks the Candidate on the forehead and sprinkles him three times.

Stolistes: 'I purify you with water.'

The Dadouchos makes a cross with Thurible and censes three times.

Dadouchos: 'I consecrate you with Fire.'

The Stolistes and Dadouchos fall back to their places in rear of the procession.

Hegemon: 'Child of Earth, twice cleansed with water and consecrated with fire, you may approach the Gate of the West.'

The Kerux leads the procession to the Throne of the Hiereus and there pausing raises the hoodwink of Candidate, who is threatened by the Hiereus with his sword.

Hiereus: 'You cannot pass by me, said the Guardian of the West until you have learned my name.'

Hegemon: (replying for Candidate): 'Your name is Darkness.'
Hiereus: 'You have known me; go forward and fear not. He who trembles at the flame and at the flood and at the shadows of the air, has no part in God.'

The Kerux replaces the Candidate's hoodwink; the Procession again moves forward, passing the Hierophant, who knocks, and the Hiereus who also knocks. When it arrives again at the N. the Kerux, turning, bars the way for the second time:

Kerux: 'Child of Earth, unpurified and unconsecrated, you cannot enter the Path of the East.'

The Stolistes and Dadouchos come forward and consecrate as before.

Stolistes: 'I purify you with Water.'
Dadouchos: 'I consecrate you with Fire.'

They retire together to the rear of the procession.

Hegemon: 'Child of Earth, thrice cleansed with water and consecrated with fire, you may approach the Gate of the East.'

The Kerux leads sunward to the Hierophant and raises hoodwink of Candidate.

Hierophant: 'You cannot pass by me, said the Guardian of the East, until you have learned my name.'
Hegemon (replying for Candidate): 'Your name is Light dawning in Darkness.'
Hierophant: 'Unbalanced Force is the squandering of life; unbalanced mercy is the passing of the will; unbalanced severity is the barrenness of the mind. You have known me; pass onward now to the Cubical Altar of created things.'

The Kerux replaces hoodwink and leads the procession to the Altar. The Hierophant leaves his Throne and passes between the Pillars with sceptre in his right hand and the Banner of the East in his left. He stops (a) between the Pillars, or (b) half way between these and the Altar, or (c) close to the East side of the Altar. The

Hiereus pauses N.W. of the Altar and the Hegemon S.W. The Candidate is placed at the W. The Kerux is immediately behind him, about half-way between the Altar and the Throne of the West. The Stolistes stands close to and due W. of the Hiereus; the Dadouchos close to and due W. of the Hegemon.

Hierophant: 'Let the Candidate kneel and pray while I invoke the Lord of the Universe'.

The Candidate is assisted accordingly. All officers and members stand.

Hierophant (turning to Altar): 'O Lord of Heaven and Earth, who didst constitute all things in Wisdom, we adore Thee and we invoke Thee. Look with approval on this Neophyte, here on his knees before Thee, and grant that he may attain the heights. Accept the pure offering of his soul aspiring unto Thee. May he prove a faithful brother among us, to the glory of thy Name and of the Hierarchies.'

The Candidate is assisted to rise. The Hierophant comes close to the Altar and lifts his sceptre above the Candidate's head. The Hiereus and Hegemon raise their sword and sceptre respectively to knot the sceptre of the Hierophant.

Hegemon: 'Inheritor of the dying world, we call you to the Living Beauty.'
Hiereus: 'Wanderer in the Wild Darkness, we call you to the Holy Light.'

At the word Light the Kerux finally removes the Hoodwink and the Sentinal turns up the Light.

Hierophant: 'We receive you into the Order of the KHABS'.
Hiereus: 'Am'
Hegemon: 'Pekht'
Hiereus: 'Konx'
Hegeman: 'Om'
Hierophant: 'Pax'
Hegemon: 'Light'
Hierophant: 'in'
Hiereus: 'Extension'

The Three Chief Officers remove their sceptres and sword from above the head of the Candidate. The Kerux passes to N.E. of Altar and raises his lamp.

Hierophant (pointing to lamp): 'In all your darkened wanderings the lamp of the Kerux went before you, signifying the Light of the Hidden Knowledge.'

All officers return to their stations, except the Hegemon. All members are seated.

Hierophant: 'Let the Neophyte be led to the East of the Altar.'

The Hegemon leads accordingly by N. to E. and places the Neophyte half way between the Altar and the Pillars, facing the East.

Hierophant: 'Honoured Hiereus, you will now impart to the Neophyte the sacred signs, token and words, together with the present password of the O=O Grade of the Order of the M∴R∴ vel G∴D∴. Place him between the Pillars and watch over his fourth and perfect Consecration.'

The Hiereus passes from his throne by N. to the Black Pillar and stands on the East side of it, facing S. The Hegemon leaves Neophyte and passing by N. takes up a similar position with regard to the White Pillar but facing N. The sword of the Hiereus is sheathed. The Hiereus turns W. and facing the Neophyte, he stands between the Pillars.

Hiereus: 'Frater Adveniat Regnum (vel alius), I will now instruct you in the secret signs, tokens and words of this Grade. The step is given by advancing your left foot—The signs are the saluting sign and the sign of silence. The first must be answered by the second. The saluting sign is given thus [Lean forward and stretch both arms out]. It alludes to your former condition when groping your way from darkness to light. The sign of silence is given by placing [the left forefinger on your lip]. It refers to the strict silence imposed by your obligation upon you concerning all proceedings of this Order. The token is [advance your left foot touching mine, toe and heel, extend your right hand to grasp mine, fail, try again and then succeed in touching the fingers only]. (The Hiereus continues to maintain the grip during the rest of his speech.) 'The Word is [Har-Par-Krat] and it is whispered in this position by separate syllables. It is the Egyptian Name of [the god of Silence] The present password is . . . It is changed at each festival of the Equinox. I now place you between the Pillars of Seth, Hermes and Solomon, in the Gateway of the Hidden Knowledge.'

He draws the Neophyte forward by the Grip until he stands between the Pillars, and then receives his sword from the Hegemon. He returns to his former position E. of and close to the Black Pillar.

Hiereus: 'Let the final and perfect consecration take place.'

The Kerux passes to the N. and there pauses until the procession is formed. The Stolistes and Dadouchos purify and consecrate the Hall as in the opening, but in place of facing the Hierophant and raising their vessels on high, they salute and then turn to consecrate the Neophyte as previously.

Stolistes: 'I purify you with Water.'

Dadouchos: 'I consecrate you by Fire.'

Again saluting the Throne, they pass by S. and W. to N., taking their places a short distance behind the Kerux.

Hierophant: 'Honoured Hegemon, I command you to remove the rope and to invest our Frater with the badge of this Grade.'

The Hegemon, passing from behind the White Pillar, hands his sceptre to the Hiereus, removes the rope and invests with the Ribbon of a Neophyte, saying:

Hegemon: 'By command of the Very Honoured Hierophant, I invest you with the Badge of this Grade. It symbolises Light dawning in Darkness.'

He returns to the White Pillar.

Hierophant: 'Let the Mystical Procession take place in the Pathway of Light.'

The Hegemon leading Neophyte—who must not pass through the pillars—takes up his position behind the Kerux. The Hiereus follows and takes his place behind the Neophyte but in front of the Stolistes and Dadouchos. When thus marshalled, the Kerux moves forward with Lamp and Wand. They pass the Hierophant once and salute. The Hiereus drops out as the Procession passes his Throne. The Hegemon circumambulates twice. The rest pass the Hierophant three times and then drop out as they reach their respective places. The Kerux and Neophyte halt on reaching a point N.W. of the Stolistes.

Hierophant: 'You will now take your seat in the North to the West of the Stolistes.'

The Kerux places the Neophyte accordingly and passes with sol round the altar to his seat. The Hegemon replaces the chair between the pillars and sits down. The Kerux restores the Rose, Lamp, Cup and Paten to Altar and returns with sol to his place. All are seated.

Hierophant: 'Frater Neophyte, at the conclusion of the Ceremony of your admission into the O=O Grade of the Honourable Order of the M.·.R.·. vel G.·.D.·., we extend to you our loving welcome upon the occasion of your admission among us, which has so far fulfilled your desire for the attainment of occult Knowledge. I will now direct your attention to the significance of the chief symbols which are met with in this Grade. The threefold cord which was bound about your waist prior to your initiation is an image of the threefold bondage of mortality, by which the once far-wandering soul has been made subject to the limitations of time and space. The Hoodwink is an image of that ignorance of mortality which has blinded man to the beauty and beatitude upon which their eyes once looked. The double Cubical Altar in the centre of the Temple is an emblem of visible Nature, concealing within itself the mysteries of all dimensions and revealing surface only to external sense. It is a double cube because the things which are below are a reflection of those which are above, as we are told by the Emerald Tablet; the world of man and woman born to sorrow is a reflection of the world above where dwell beings created for joy. The Altar is black because the fires of created things arise from darkness and obscurity, which Divine Beings unfold in an element of Light. The White Triangle is placed on the Altar as an image of the Triune Light which moved in the Darkness, forming the world in Darkness and out of Darkness. There are two contending powers and one always uniting them. These three are imaged in the triple flame of ones being and in the triplicity of the world of sense. They are the Triad of Life. The Red Cross above the Triangle is a symbol of him who is unfolded in the Light.'

The Hierophant rises and extends his arms in the form of a Cross.

Hierophant: 'Glory be to Thee, Father Almighty, for Thy Glory flows out rejoicing to the ends of the Earth.'

The Hierophant reseats himself.

Hierophant: 'The mystical words KHABS, AM, PEKHT are Ancient Egyptian and the original of the Greek KONX, OM, PAX, which were uttered in the Eleusinian Mysteries. They refer to the same mode of light as that which is symbolised by the staff of the Kerux. To the East of the Cubical Altar are the Pillars which are referred by our secret tradition to Seth, Hermes and Solomon. They bear certain hieroglyphical texts from the XVIIth and CXXVth chapters of the Ritual of the Dead. They are the door-posts of the Gateway of the Hidden Wisdom, they are the emblems of eternal equilibrium, of the dual powers of day and night, love and hatred, severity and mercy, fixed and volatile, work and rest, the subtle force of the loadstone, with its dual polarity, and the eternal outpouring and inpouring of the heart of God. The Lamps that burn with a veiled light upon their summits point out that the Path of the Hidden Knowledge is the straight and narrow way between them, unlike the Path of Nature, which is a continual undulation, the coiling and uncoiling of the serpent. It was for this that I passed between the pillars when you were restored to the Light and for this also that you were placed between them to receive the perfect consecration. My Throne at the Gate of the East is the place of the Rising Sun. The Throne of the Hiereus at the Gate of the West is the place of the Guardian against those multitudes which sleep through light and waken in twilight. The chair of the Hegemon who is seated between the Pillars, with mitre-headed sceptre, is the place of balanced power betwixt the ultimate Light and the ultimate Darkness. These meanings are further indicated by our insignia and the colours of our Robes. The Wand of the Kerux is a beam from the Light of the Hidden Wisdom, and his Lantern is an emblem of the Ever-Burning Lamp borne by the Guardian of the Mysteries. The seal of the Stolistes at the Gate of the North, signifying cold, is the place of the Guardian of the cauldron and the well of water. The seal of the Dadouchos in the South, signifying heat, is the place of the Guardian of the Lake of Fire and the Burning Bush.' A pause.

Hierophant: 'Frater Kerux, I command you to declare that the Neophyte has been regularly initiated into the Mysteries of the O=O Grade.'

Kerux (advancing to Right Front of Hierophant and raising his Wand): 'In the name of Him who works in silence and whom only silence can express, and by command of the Very Honoured Hierophant, hear ye all: I proclaim that A.B., who will be known hereafter among us by the motto Adveniat Regnum (vel alius) has been duly admitted to the O=O Grade and is a Neophyte in the Order of the M.·.R vel G.·.D.·.'

The Kerux returns to his place saluting the Hierophant as he passes.

Hiereus: 'Frater Adveniat Regnum (vel alius), Let me exhort you ever to remember your obligation of secrecy in this Order. There is strength in silence; the seed of Wisdom is sown therein and it grows in darkness and mystery. Remember the secret law of equilibrium, without which the virtues themselves become evils. Remember that all religions are to be held in reverence for all are rays of that ineffable Light which you are seeking. Remember the Penalty which awaits the breaker of his oath. Remember the Mystery which you have received. Remember that things divine are not for those who understand the body alone for only those who are lightly armed will attain to the summit. Remember that God alone is our light, the bestower of perfect Illumination. No mortal power can do more than bring you to the pathway of

Wisdom. Honour Him who could, if it so pleased Him, make it known to the heart of a child. The ends of the Earth are swept by the borders of his garment of flames. From Him proceed all things and unto Him all things return. Therefore we invoke Him; therefore even the Banner of the East falls in adoration before Him. Remember, lastly, that perseverance conquers all difficulties and do not be daunted by those which await you in the pursuit of the Hidden Knowledge.'

Hierophant: 'Before your advancement to the next Grade of this Order a familiarity with the elementary symbols of our science will be required of you. The papers containing them may be obtained on application to the Cancellarius, with whom you should communicate in writing when you have attained proficiency in the subjects. Your knowledge will then be tested and if found satisfactory you are at liberty to apply for admission to the next grade. Remember, however, that without a dispensation from the Second Order no person can be admitted or advanced in any Grade of the First Order.'

The Minutes of the previous meeting are then read and signed.

The Closing

Hierophant: (knocks once)
Kerux (passing to N.W. of Hierophant's Throne and raising Wand): 'Hekas, Hekas, este bebeloi.'

He returns to his place by E.S. and W., saluting as he passes the Throne of the Hierophant.

Hierophant: '*Fratres* and *Sorores* of the Isis Urania Temple of the M.·.R.·. vel G.·.D.·. assist me to close this Hall of the Neophytes (knocks).

All stand up

Hierophant: '*Frater Kerux*, see that the Temple is properly guarded."
This is done as in Opening, the Kerux knocking at the Temple door from within and the Sentinel replying from without.

Kerux: 'Very Honoured Hierophant, the Temple is properly guarded.'

Hierophant: 'Honoured Hiereus, assure yourself that all present have witnessed the *M.·.R.·.*'

Hiereus: 'Fratres and Sorores, give the signs of a Neophyte ... Very Honoured Hierophant, all present have witnessed the *M.·.R.·.*'

Hierophant: (with sign): 'Let the Temple be cleansed with Water and consecrated by Fire.'

The Stolistes purifies as at the Opening.

Stolistes: 'I purify with Water.'

The Dadouchos consecrates as at Opening.

Dadouchos: 'I consecrate by Fire.'
Hierophant: 'Let the Mystical Reverse Procession take place in the Pathway of Light.'

The Kerux passes by W. to S. The Hegemon passes by N. to W. and S. The Hiereus passes by W. to S. The Dadouchos takes his place on the right of Stolistes. The Neophyte is directed to a position in front of the Stolistes and Dadouchos. When the procession is thus formed, the Kerux leads by E. and all salute in passing the Throne of the Hierophant: as the procession passes the Throne of the Hiereus he returns thereto. As it passes the Throne of the Hierophant for the second time, the Hegemon retires to his place. The others circumambulate and salute for the third time, each dropping out of the procession as it reaches his own place.

Hierophant: 'The Mystical Reverse Procession is accomplished in commemoration of the Fading Light ... Let us adore the Light of the Universe.'

All turn E. maintaining the Sign of the Grade until the Adoration is over.

Hierophant: 'Holy art Thou, O Lord of the Universe! Holy are

Thou whom Nature hath not formed! Holy art Thou who workest in silence and nought but silence can express.'

All face as before.

Hierophant:'Let us now partake in silence of the Mystical Repast composed of the symbols of the Four Elements and remember our vow of secrecy.'

The Hierophant, leaving his Insignia, goes to the West of the Altar and, facing E. raises the Mystical Rose, saying:

Hierophant: 'I invite you to inhale with me the perfume of this Rose, as a symbol of Air'; (placing his hands over the fire) 'to feel the warmth of this sacred Fire'; (partakes of bread and salt) 'to eat of this bread and of this salt as types of Earth'; (raises chalice) 'and, finally to drink with me of this Wine, the consecrated emblem of Elemental Waters.'

He passes to E. of Altar with Sol and administers the Mystical Repast to the Senior Chief, raising and handing him each of the elements in turn. The saluting Sign is not made by any one during this ceremony. The Chiefs partake in their order and are followed by the officers from the Hiereus to the Dadouchos. The Sentinel commemorates in accordance with his grade in the Order. When the Dadouchos has placed himself E. of the Altar, the Hierophant says:

Hierophant: 'Let all Members below the Grade of the Portal be seated.'

The 5=6 Members communicate in whatever order they happen to be placed in the Hall, beginning with the one nearest to the Hierophant on the left and working round by S.W. and N. to the one nearest the Hierophant on his right. Each member throughout the Ceremony offers the elements in turn to the one who comes after him and for this purpose passes to E. of Altar. He then returns to his place, moving round the Altar with Sol and so resuming his seat. When all 5=6 Members have thus communicated and the last is standing at the E. of the Altar, the Hierophant says:

Hierophant: 'Let all Members of the 4=7 Grade now rise.'

They rise and partake in the same order and manner as the 5 = 6.

Hierophant: 'Let all Members of the 3=8 Grade now rise.'

They rise and partake as before.

Hierophant: 'Let all Members of the 2=9 Grade now rise.'

They rise and partake as before.

Hierophant: 'Let all Members of the 1=10 Grade now rise.'

They rise and partake as before.

Hierophant: 'Let all Neophytes now rise.'

They rise and partake as before. When the last Neophyte is placed at the E. of the Altar the Kerux comes up without Insignia and communicates; but when he is handed the Chalice he consumes the Wine and holding the Cup on high turns it upside down and cries with a loud voice:

Kerux: 'It is finished.'

All rise. The Kerux restores the Chalice to the Altar and returns to his place.

Hierophant: (knocks): 'Tetelestai!'
Hiereus: (knocks once).

All give sign.

Hierophant: 'May what we have received sustain us in our search for the Quintessence the Stone of the Philosophers, true Wisdom and Perfect Happiness—the *Summum Bonum.*'
Hierophant (knocks): '*Khabs*'
Hiereus (knocks): '*Am*'
Hegemon (knocks): '*Pekht*'

Hiereus (knocks): '*Konx*'
Hegemon (knocks): '*Om*'
Hierophant (knocks): '*Pax*'
Hegemon (knocks): '*Light*'
Hierophant (knocks): '*in*'
Hiereus (knocks): '*Extension*'

If the hall is not reserved exclusively for Temple meetings, it should be purified by the Lesser Ritual of the Pentagram, performed by the Hierophant with his sceptre so soon as the Members are assembled. In case the Hall is not duly oriented the following Prayer should be recited by the Hierophant before the formal Opening but after the rehearsal of the Lesser Ritual. For this purpose the Hierophant should stand facing the true East, between that point and the Altar.

Prayer

Creator of the Universe, Lord of the Visible World, who hast by thy supreme Power set bounds to the magnitude thereof and hast, in particular, conferred special attributes to those limitations, Grant, we beseech Thee, that whatever mystic and hidden virtue abides in the Radiant East, the Dayspring of Light and the Font of Life, may in answer to this our prayer be here and now conferred upon the Throne of the Hierophant of this Temple, who is the emblem of that Dawning Golden Light which shall illuminate the Pathway of the Unknown and shall, in fine, lead us even unto the attainment of the Quintessence, the Stone of the Wise, True Wisdom and Perfect Happiness.

Appendix D

The Condition needed for Entry into the Second Order

by

S[apere] A[ude]

Your instructions in the several Grades of the 'G.D. in the Outer' have been intellectual exercises in the symbolism of medieval and ancient occult science: they have been to many of you apparently barbarous and without use. Permit me to assure you that the knowledge lectures contain only such information as is truly valuable and indeed quite necessary, before further progress is made. As one passes on into higher grades every statement made in them and all the wisdom partially revealed in the Rituals, will be found to form an essential whole of a concrete and finely designed system of Philosophy. You have been informed that the Chiefs have invited you to make further progress, but let me beg of you not to accept that invitation until you feel confident that not only the facts as arrayed have been appreciated by you, but that in addition, you have in your mind, sorted and recorded them, and have found a certain coherence between the many symbols laid before you. But it is not only an intellectual study of these pages which is needed; it is hoped that you have, to some extent, clothed the dry bones with life and force and have been able to spiritualize and idealize the names and forms and symbols laid before you; for it is especially to the psychic and then to the spiritual places of thought and formation that you will be in future led. Intellectual grasp *alone*, will prove but a broken reed in your hands, in the higher grades: no real progress will be made unless you cultivate the ideals of objects rather than their materiality, and unless you can realize the forces which surround you, which you absorb, and which you may learn to wield. For this new development of yourself, two requirements are essential; a *Clean Life*, and an *Indomitable Will*; if you have these two essentials all other things shall be added unto them.

By a clean life passed in a whirl of sin and folly I mean that you shall formulate an ideal of rectitude of life and actions, and a purity of thought and intention. No one can do more in this direction, than he can; but you can do more than you have—unless indeed you have no need to come to us. In all your endeavours—be honest to yourself, and don't wink at your faults; recognize them, condemn them and pass them by, never brood over them. Do every action for a good and worthy purpose, and when done never mind the result. If you have done a good deed and evil has resulted, trouble not, you are not the ruling providence; and you cannot expect to understand all the interactions between yourself and others, which some call Providence, others fate, others destiny and other Karma. If your intentions have been good, the result cannot fail to be good to you, upon one plane or the other. If you carry out this dictum you will have much more time to spend with energy upon other works, than will those who waste time and force upon regrets, which are alike useless and vain, and a besetting weakness to neglect of action—to passivity, and to personal decay.

Never attempt to make anyone think you are better than you are; and don't yourself think you are better than you are, self-hypocrisy is a crime, hypocrisy to others is only a fraud. Temperance, Continence and self-sacrifice are all grand characteristics, and form part of a Higher Life, but Self-Gratulation upon their acquisition renders them valueless in your career, and they become but as tinkling cymbals instead of a sound of music from the spheres. Modern civilization and the manners of good society are things rotten at the core, and to be unconventional will be a sign of improvement, if you desert common rule for a *better* practice; but beware lest you desert some commonly approved rule or practice only for a personal fancy—for of this new departure you have had no experience, and if that thing were practised by all, an even worse result might occur. It is on such a point as this, that the experience gained by those who have already sought that Path, may avail you.

I must warn you that you cannot be orthodox as orthodoxy now goes, retire at once if you must be so; and this chiefly because the key note of the faith of the nation in which you have been bred is 'Trust in another'. By self-Reliance alone, can any progress be made. An Hermetic Master is a Guide post, not a walking stick. No senior among us will let you lean on him; he will only show a few steps of the way, he has passed and you must not pass even that way if your higher senses tell you that such are not for you: for the paths are many but there is one goal to which all good paths lead. Many paths are good, and end in happiness which is Wisdom; but every good path is toilsome, steep and often rugged; and if you find yourself treading a path of thought and action, which is pleasant and easy—Beware thereof, and take counsel with your Higher Self, lest you are self deceived and you are but wandering in a labyrinth with flowery borders which conceal perchance many noxious animals, snares, and foot holes. Be not ambitious in the world's sense; strive for *self* culture, not that you may be able to surpass your fellow, but work as they do, who are ambitious. Sin and even death are alike avoidable,—the latter within limits.

'Man doth not yield himself unto the Angels nor unto death utterly—save only through the weakness of his feeble will'. Cultivate a healthy mind and body, and so alone can you cultivate a powerful Will: Will is a plant of illimitable growth; but it will not grow wild, it must be forced. Never drift with the tide, decide upon every occasion, always act—never suffer a thing to occur. Every failure to stand on your own basis, every time you lean on another, every hope for others' help will sap the foundations of Will Power.

Look unto the Master Jesus, if you will, with reverence, with admiration, with gratitude, in that his history, his life and his teachings have led you to recognize holiness and purity, but look not to him, or any other, to save you—if you won't save yourself. He has shewn an excellent path, attempt it, but do not cling to his garments, he is an 'example' not a beast of burden.

Substituted service is a weakness and a failure. Salvation by faith alone in any God or any man is a chimera, a fatal delusion.

If these sayings are hard unto you—come not with us; delay,— in hope of increased strength and clear insight into analogies between Man the Microcosm and the Universal Macrocosm, which passes up to the Divinest Essence we can conceive, *and* beyond it.

In the Second Order, we are still very human but not only

human—we are *attempting* to be ultra-human, i.e. divine. If you enter there, you must be in thought and practice like an Angel, one who has passed beyond contract worship. Unless while with us you can conceive and act as both a sister and a brother at once, you will become a curse to yourself and a stumbling block unto us, unless you can forget your sex,—by the holy Tetragrammaton I beseech you to be absent. We do not ask you to be unsexed in your private life, *that* is a stage necessary only in a far advanced grade, to which few may reach, but in our Order this qualification is an absolute necessity or you will get no encouragement to proceed farther than the threshold. If you can promise this attitude, you *may* attempt; beware of a first failure, it may end in your failure in this incarnation, and in others: but it *might* be overcome.

When I think of my experience, I am tempted to say, Retire while it is yet time. The occult burden is not light, it is not easy to bear, be warned in time, for the higher you rise—the more terrible the fall—if you should fall.

So far—S.A.

Appendix E

Ritual U: The Secret Wisdom of the Lesser World or Microcosm Which is Man

Part 5:

Of Travelling in the Spirit Vision

The Symbol, Place, direction or plane being known, whereon it is desired to act, a thought-ray as before is sent unto the corresponding part of the Sphere of Sensation; and thence, by drawing a basis of action from the refined Astral Light of the Sphere of Sensation of the Nephesh (the Soul as Vital Essence), the thought-ray is sent like an *arrow* from a *bow* right *through* the circumference of the Sphere of Sensation, direct unto the place desired. Arrived here a Sphere of Astral Light is formed by the agency of the Lower Will illuminated by the Higher Will, and acting through the Spiritual Consciousness by reflection along the thought-ray; and this sphere of Astral Light is partly drawn from the Nephesh and partly from the surrounding atmosphere.

This sphere being formed, a *simulacrum* of the Person of the Skryer is *reflected* into it along the thought-ray, and the united Consciousness is then projected therein. This sphere is therefore a duplicate, by reflection, of the Sphere of Sensation.

As it is said:— 'Believe thyself to be in a place, and thou art there.'

In this Astral Projection, however, a certain part of the Consciousness must remain in Body to protect the Thought-Ray beyond the limits of the Sphere of Sensation (as well as the sphere itself at that point of departure of the Thought-Ray) from attack by any hostile force, so that the Consciousness in this projection is not quite so strong as the Consciousness when concentrated in the Natural Body in ordinary life.

The return taketh place with a *reversal* of this process; and, save to persons whose Nephesh and Physical Body are exceptionally strong and healthy, the whole operation of 'Skrying' and Travelling in the Spirit-Vision is of course fatiguing.

Also there is another mode of Astral projection which can be used by the more practised and advanced Adept. This consisteth in forming first a sphere from his own Sphere of Sensation, casting his reflection therein, and then projecting this whole sphere to the desired place as in the previous method. But this is not easy to be done by any but the practised operator.

Thus far regarding Skrying and Travelling in the Spirit Vision.

Appendix F

Astral Travelling

No. 2

The Sword

On Thursday, 20th December, 1900, Soror Deo Date and a group of students met at 36 B[lythe] R[oad] in order to investigate clairvoyantly the symbolism of the Sword. We sat in a semi-circle at the north side of the Altar, facing the South, when Mars was in Virgo at the time. Deo Date then made the Invoking Hexagrams of Mars round the room, and the Pentagram of Virgo and the Mars symbol towards the South. We then mentally formulated the Hexagram of Mars in red light at that point of the compass. The upper triangle appeared flaming, and an armed figure of somewhat earthy type seemed to look through it. The earthiness we ascribed to the fact that the sign Virgo had been invoked. The figure probably represented the energy of Mars (who is the planet of outward manifestation) bringing the hidden life of the earth to the surface, only to be destroyed and consumed as soon as it reached outward perfection, as in time of harvest.

We did not stop to examine this figure much, but went through the Hex. astrally and found ourselves in a region of flames. There we invoked the White Light, vibrating the Names and holding our Swords towards heaven. This had the effect of attracting a rush of energy, Deo Date feeling it chiefly in her right arm, showing it to be an energy impelling to action. A gigantic, mail clad Angel appeared, with winged helmet, and great flame-coloured wings from his shoulders. There was some diversity of opinion concerning his Sword. One Frater thought that the Angel (who was evidently Phaleg) had the hilt in one hand and the point in the other, while the blade seemed to encircle the universe. Another Frater saw it as the Flaming Sword. Others of us saw it as a straight shaft of white flame. We all held the points of our Swords to the Angel's breast from which rushed such tremendous force that our arms received a sort of electric shock. Behind the figure was a great Sun, with which it was connected by a ray of white light. From this white ray he seemed to extract the red light with which he shone. It seemed as if the highest part of the Mars force was in reality solar.

We now gave the full Lux Signs. At once a change came over the figure. It was wrapped in great sweeping black clouds and disappeared from view. In the midst of the darkness an altar appeared. One Frater saw a flaming heart upon it, but most of us saw rather a river of blood—red and rushing, giving the impression of life, not death. Its source seemed to be above the altar somewhere, but unseen. At the point where it came into view was white light, from which it seemed to derive its energy, though at the same time it imparted to it some of its own, for from the point of junction between the blood and the light sprang petal-shaped white flames outlined with gold.

(*Note*. I am afraid I have forgotten what the others saw here, and must add it in afterwards. S.L.)

We now gathered round the altar which appeared as a cauldron full of a red blood-like, or rather wine-like, fluid, with fiery serpents darting through it, as if they were the vehicles of its life. Then we vibrated the Names and rose in what we thought at first was a blade-shaped shaft of White Light. Afterwards it appeared more like the arrow part of the symbol of Mars, while we seemed to rise from the circle below. It seemed to represent the aspiring part of the nature of Mars, and on a lower plane might symbolize the ambition which is a leading characteristic of those born under this planet.

Strangely enough the figure we encountered at the end of our flight was not martial, but ecclesiastical. To some of us he appeared like the Pope in full pontifical robes, white, with triple crown on head, and triple cross in right hand, but to one soror at least he was robed like the Pope on less solemn occasions, with a short red cape over a white robe, and a red skull-cap on head. In his left hand was a half-closed book. Under his feet was a dark cave, which seemed to hide some mystery. This may possibly have represented the Vault on a higher plane, as the Hierophant naturally represents the Perfected Adept, the 'Risen Christ', triumphant over 'death'. We seemed to have been led through the path of Mars on to a solar plane. All the planets are but rays, or differentiations of the Sun, it is true, but some special teaching was evidently to be given us by this abrupt transition from Mars, the planet of outward expulsion and destruction, to the Sun, who symbolizes the all-attracting, inward-drawing centre, and who is the planet of Life and Resurrection. The Tarot symbol of Mars is very suggestive in this connection, also the alchemical meaning of iron, which has the same symbol as Mars, and is said to be corrosive externally, but solar *internally*.

(Note. I think it was at this point that we asked for information concerning the hilt of the Sword, which is like a reversed cross when the point is raised. All I can remember is that the cross bar was a guard against the higher forces, preventing the escape into spirit of the material before it had finished its career in the outer. So that the sword held point downwards cannot be altogether an evil symbol; for though it invokes the evil demons, it does so by the power of the spirit, which it seems to be the office of Mars to project to the outward confines of matter. Its path is one of enlightenment as well as destruction. Christ (the Hierophant) came not to bring peace, but a Sword upon earth.)

Written out by Soror Servio Liberaliter

Appendix G

The Manifesto of 24 July 1903

We, the undersigned, Members of the Order R.R. et A.C., having been asked to state the grounds on which we demand independence, hereby affirm as follows: –

We object to return to the status quo ante 1890 along the lines proposed by the Draft Constitution 1903.

We will not be committed definitely to any expression of opinion regarding our past connection with a Third Order.

We object to the principle of practical examination within the Second Order.

We object to the continued use of the original defective rituals and we require them re-edited in strict accordance with the cipher manuscripts.

We are of opinion that Grades within the Second Order should either cease or advancement therein should take place otherwise than by the present system of examination, more especially in practical subjects. We do not consider that any person competent to confer the higher grades is now amongst us. We regard the examination of one 5 to 6 member by another as childish. We confirm clause 9 of the Draft Constitution 1903, with such modifications as may seem desirable. The clause is as follows:

Having regard to the fact that the secret knowledge of the Second Order has been and is in possession of certain Adepti independently of grade and that for the present the side grade of Theoricus has no special knowledge of importance the existence of grades shall cease and there shall be an absolute equality of membership apart from official position; any special knowledge of the Theoricus Grade shall be attainable by 5 to 6 members as such.

We consider that the expectation of an established or renewed connection with a Third Order cannot be too carefully controlled and if such a connection should be affirmed by any Chief or 5 to 6 Adept we do not regard the Theorici as the sole or necessarily the best judges of the evidence.

We object to the statements which have been circulated by which we are represented as having affirmed the restoration of the status quo ante 1890. At the Annual Meeting in 1902, a temporary and experimental coalition was formed to last till May 4, 1903, to prevent the entire paralysis of all business, but the two sections of the Order were obviously not in agreement then and they are not in agreement now.

We consider that all in our power should be done to corroborate and extend our knowledge and not to restrict it within the present narrow limits. We consider that special attention should be given to historical and mystical research.

We hold that the Order should be reconstituted and desire to reconstitute it on its original basis prior to the ascendency obtained by a single Chief. The Order was established about 1885 by Chiefs who were Masons and possessed high grades in the Masonic fraternity. If these Chiefs were warranted by a Third Order, they were in our opinion warranted as Masons. The Order at that time was ruled from within a body in which the Masonic qualification was required of joining members. The Order in respect of its rituals as well as of its government was Masonic at that period and is still Masonic by its rituals. It has become divorced from Masonry solely through the dissensions of the original Chiefs. The period of harmony and progress was the Masonic period and the difficulties began when the Chiefs forgot that they were Masons. We affirm the necessity of restoring the Masonic rapport by electing certain Masons as Chiefs and encouraging, as regards men, the admission of Masons rather than non-Masons to the Outer and Inner Grades of the Order. We believe also that the extension of our knowledge and the communication with a Third Order must be sought in those fraternities which some of us know and others believe to exist behind Masonry.

We affirm that the earliest status of the Order was mystical and that the trend of the Order practice towards the lower occultism rose with the rise and grew with the growth of the ascendency of a single Chief. Attention was originally paid to the mystic way, more especially when the studies were chiefly directed by S.A. We desire to give prominence to this method of progress.

We are of opinion that our objects will be best attained by the constitution of an independent branch of the R.R. et A.C. working under a Masonic regime and that this course does not involve hostility to those whose requirements are met by the practical part of the Order knowledge. We have no idea of excluding women from membership or from office within the Order, apart from the Masonic Chieftainship, which is a business and working headship. We believe that our scheme is calculated to increase the number of male members and thus ensure that equality of the sexes; and we affirm in conclusion our intention of insisting on the literal fulfilment of all our requirements for which purpose We Hereby Declare Our Independence From The Date Hereof To Be Reconsidered If Our Demands Are Granted.

VIRTUTE ORTA OCCIDUNT RARIUS

MAWAHAHU THESI

SACRAMENTUM REGIS

VIGILATE

A POSSE AD ESSE

SHEMEBER

CAUSA SCIENTIAE

SILENTIO

PERSEVERA

ALTA PETO

TEMPUS OMNIA REVELAT

VOLO ASPIRARE

Appendix H

Constitution of the R.R. et A.C.

(Proclaimed at the Meeting held on 7 November 1903)

1. The name of the order shall be the Independent and Rectified Order R.R. et A.C.
2. The Order is the custodian of certain knowledge a part of which only can be found in printed books or known manuscripts. There is further knowledge obtainable along the same lines.
3. The Independent and Rectified Order believes that there is a higher or mystical sense of the entire Order knowledge.
4. It affirms individually and collectively its earnest desire for advancement in spiritual knowledge by which alone a connection can be established with Masters in Secret Science.
5. The original connection of the R.R. et A.C. with such Masters under the name of the Third Order is a matter of opinion but the existence of special knowledge within the Second Order, however derived, is not a matter of opinion and is its title to continuation and diffusion.
6. The Chiefs of the Second Order shall be Master Masons of the 3rd, Degree in accordance with the tradition of the Order holding under the Mother Grand Lodge of England or some other Grand Lodge recognized by her.
7. All authority within the Order is vested in the three Chiefs. The existing Chiefs are VIRTUTE ORTA OCCIDUNT RARIUS, MAWAHANU THESI, SACRAMENTUM

REGIS. In the event of the death or demission of a Chief his place shall be filled by another Mason from within the ranks of the Second Order.

8. The power of appointment in this case shall rest with the remaining Chiefs.

9. The special Grade of Theoricus is abrogated and the knowledge possessed thereby is placed at the disposition of the Second Order as a whole.

10. There are no examinations within the 5 6 Grade which is the sole Grade of the Second Order.

11. The advancement of new members in the knowledge possessed by the Second Order takes place at the discretion of the Chiefs.

12. The instruction of new members may be delegated to experienced Fratres or Sorores at the discretion of the Chiefs.

13. The V. H. Soror VIGILATE is hereby appointed Keeper of the archives of the Independent and Rectified Order with the title of Recorder.

14. The V. H. Soror SHEMEBER is appointed the Bursar of the Order.

15. The Order shall as soon as possible acquire a permanent habitation which shall be placed under the control of a librarian to be hereafter appointed.

16. There shall be a special meeting of the Order in January of each year when the Recorder shall present the Report of the progress of the Order and the Treasurer the financial statement.

17. All disputes and complaints shall be in the sole jurisdiction of the Chiefs and in the case of differences between members they shall be determined as privately as possible.

18. Every member of the Independent and Rectified Order shall be honourably bound to abide by the constitution and the regulations.

19. Simple resignation or demission from the Second Order shall not of itself involve the forfeiture of manuscripts. All manuscripts are however held by members at the will of the Chiefs.

20. Expulsions can only take place by fiat of the Chiefs or at their discretion by a vote in the Vault of the Adepts with a 3. 4ths majority, notice having been sent seven days before the meeting to every member.

21. The C. C. Ceremony will be retained but will undergo a

certain slight revision in order to bring it more into harmony with the traditions of past ages.

22. The subscription of the Second Order is (Xs) per annum which can be remitted at the discretion of the Chiefs in certain cases.

23. The Trustees of all the Properties of the Inner and Outer Orders are MAWAHANU THESI and VIGILATE.

24. The regular meetings of the Second Order are the first Saturday in January, April, July and September at such times and places as may be appointed.

Select Bibliography

The greater part of the rituals of the Order are contained in the following:

Regardie, F. Israel, *The Golden Dawn. An Account of the Teachings, Rites and Ceremonies of the Order of the Golden Dawn.* Chicago, Aries Press, 1937–1940 4 volumes. (A revised edition published by Llewellyn Publications (1971) is available from Thorsons Publishers)

Torrens, R. G., *The Secret Rituals of the Golden Dawn.* Wellingborough, Aquarian Press, 1973 (The rituals printed date from 1897 but Torrens' own text is historically inaccurate and, in the case of the list of members and their mottoes, wholly unreliable.)

Mathers, S. L. M. and Others, *Astral Projection, Ritual Magic and Alchemy. Being Hitherto Unpublished Golden Dawn Material. Edited and Introduced by Francis King.* Spearman, 1971 (Comprising twenty of the 'Flying Rolls' plus other papers)

The history of the Order is given substantially in the following:

Colquhoun, I., *Sword of Wisdom, MacGregor Mathers and 'The Golden Dawn'.* Spearman, 1975 (Important for the later history, but many biographical details are inaccurate)

Howe, Ellic, *The Magicians of the Golden Dawn. A Documentary History of a Magical Order 1887–1923.* Routledge & Kegan Paul, 1972 (The definitive history)

King, Francis, *Ritual Magic in England 1887 to the Present Day.* Spearman, 1970 (Entertaining, and with information on modern offshoots not found elsewhere – but not wholly reliable)

Regardie, F. Israel, *My Rosicrucian Adventure. A contribution to a recent phase of the History of Magic, and a study in the technique of Theurgy. Second and revised Edition.* St. Paul, Minn., Llewellyn, 1971. (The author's account of his personal involvement with the Order)

(Stoddart, Miss C. M.), *Light-bearers of Darkness. By Inquire Within. For some years a Ruling Chief of the Mother Temple of the Stella Matutina and R.R. et A.C.* Boswell, 1930 (A major source for the history of the Stella Matutina, but marred by the author's obsession with the 'Jewish Peril')

Waite, A. E., *Shadows of Life and Thought. A Retrospective Review in the Form of Memoirs.* Selwyn and Blount, 1938 (A personal account of the Order up to 1903 but, as with all such versions, not entirely accurate)

Harper, G. M., *Yeats's Golden Dawn.* Macmillan, 1974. (The principal source for Yeats' involvement with the Order, and having highly important Appendices of original documents)

Index